T0291230

# Team Academy:
# Leadership and Teams

Within Entrepreneurship Education, Team Academy is seen by some as an innovative pedagogical model that enhances social connectivity, as well as experiential, student-centred, and team-based learning. It also creates spaces for transformative learning to occur.

In this book, the third book in the Routledge Focus on Team Academy series, the contributors explore the concepts of leadership and teams in the context of TA. Topics including the way in which learners attempt to navigate the complexity of leadership and team dynamics, while understanding their place and impact on the processes involved, will be examined.

This book is aimed at academics, practitioners, and learners engaged in the Team Academy methodology, pedagogy, and model, as well as those interested in the area of entrepreneurial team learning. Readers will be inspired to innovate in their delivery methodologies and to explore learning-by-doing approaches to creating value. The book also aims to challenge the discourse around entrepreneurship and entrepreneurial activities, offering insights, research, stories, and experiences from those learning and working in the Team Academy approach.

**Dr Elinor Vettraino** is Head Coach and Programme Director of the Business Enterprise Development Portfolio at Aston University, UK.

**Dr Berrbizne Urzelai** is Team Coach and Senior Lecturer in areas of International Management and Entrepreneurship at the University of the West of England, UK.

# Routledge Focus on Team Academy
**Series Editors** – Berrbizne Urzelai and Elinor Vettraino

Higher Education organizations (HE) operate in an environment that continuously pushes towards innovation by educators. From this perspective, Team Academy is seen as an innovative pedagogical model that enhances social connectivity, as well as experiential, student-centred, and team-based learning. It also creates spaces for transformative learning to occur.

Since its creation in Finland in 1993, the number of institutions adopting this approach has been expanding in many parts of Europe and beyond, and it is increasingly attracting the interest of organizations that want to adopt a model that emphasizes the transversal competences and skills acquired by its entrepreneurial learners. The aim of this series is to compile the different research, experiences, and stories about the Team Academy phenomenon throughout its worldwide network.

The audience of the books is multidisciplinary, directed to academics and practitioners. Entrepreneurial education and research has traditionally been focused on the individual entrepreneur. However, in the current business scenario, entrepreneurs' teamwork efforts, social capital, and networking skills are essential to face the entrepreneurial issues and challenges that they currently face. The books adopt a Team Academy pedagogical approach that focuses on critical factors such as team and experiential learning, leadership, or entrepreneurial mindset, which makes this collection a key information source for those looking at new directions of entrepreneurship education and practice.

**Team Academy and Entrepreneurship Education**
*Edited by Elinor Vettraino and Berrbizne Urzela*

**Team Academy in Practice**
*Edited by Berrbizne Urzelai and Elinor Vettraino*

**Team Academy Leadership and Teams**
*Edited by Elinor Vettraino and Berrbizne Urzelai*

**Team Academy in Diverse Settings**
*Edited by Berrbizne Urzelai and Elinor Vettraino*

# Team Academy:
# Leadership and Teams

**Edited by Elinor Vettraino and
Berrbizne Urzelai**

LONDON AND NEW YORK

First published 2022
by Routledge
605 Third Avenue, New York, NY 10158

and by Routledge
2 Park Square, Milton Park, Abingdon, Oxon, OX14 4RN

Routledge is an imprint of the Taylor & Francis Group,
an informa business

*Library of Congress Cataloging-in-Publication Data*
A catalog record for this title has been requested

ISBN: 978-0-367-75597-3 (hbk)
ISBN: 978-0-367-75598-0 (pbk)
ISBN: 978-1-003-16312-1 (ebk)

DOI: 10.4324/9781003163121

Typeset in Times New Roman
by MPS Limited, Dehradun

*For those who lead themselves and others with passion, integrity, and care.*

– Dr Elinor Vettraino

*For Scion and Valor members, who taught me what team coaching is.*

– Dr Berrbizne Urzelai

# Contents

# Figures

# Tables

# Acknowledgements

We would like to thank all of the contributors for their stories, and the learners, researchers, and practitioners for their commitment to exploration and learning-by-doing. Without them, this book wouldn't have been possible.

Dr Elinor Vettraino and Dr Berrbizne Urzelai

# Contributors

**Izsakun Agirre Aranburu, Professor of Marketing, Faculty of Business, Mondragon University, Spain**. Izaskun Agirre, PhD, is a professor of marketing at the Faculty of Business, Mondragon University, where she also coordinates the MBA–Executive jointly with the provincial chamber of commerce. Nowadays she also works as PhD program's coordinator. She has been chairperson of the Department of Marketing and Educational Innovation at the Faculty. She is a member of the research group on business development and her research areas include customer experience, cooperative business, and digital experience. She has published articles in journals including the *Journal Business Ethics*, the *Review of Radical Political Economics*, and the *Annals of Public and Cooperative Economics*.

**Colin Dargent, Graduate, Team Academy Strasbourg, Strasbourg School of Management, France**. Colin lives in France, in Lille, and is currently a student in human resources. Colin also works for 109L', Innovation Dans Les Veines, as a community of practice project manager. He completed the Team Academy BA in Strasbourg between 2016 and 2019. This experience allowed him to discover entrepreneurship, teamwork, leadership, and also the importance of learning. This is a central issue for companies because it reflects their ability to evolve and adapt.

**Hugo Gaggiotti, Associate Professor, University of West of England, UK**. Hugo Gaggiotti is Associate Professor at the University of the West of England, Bristol, UK. The focus of his writing is on the intersections between professional mindsets and how organizations could contribute to the construction of vulnerability in particular contexts of repetitive change, displacement, transfiguration, and liminality, like international borderlands, multinational assembly plants, and ephemeral project-based work. His work has appeared in a range of interdisciplinary journals and his books include *Organizational Ethnography: An Experiential and Practical Guide* (in press) and *Origins of Organising* (2019).

**Marcellin Grandjean, Learning Team Coach, Team Academy Strasbourg, Strasbourg School of Management, France.** Marcellin Grandjean is Learning Team Coach in the Team Entrepreneur programme at the Strasbourg School of Management. He is the co-founder of the Mana Mana Cooperative which disseminates the Team Academy approach in organizations and education. Personally, he explores the conditions that allow the emergence of action in projects. His motto is: whatever happens, it will happen!

**Carol Jarvis, Professor in Knowledge Exchange and Innovation, Bristol Business School, University of West of England, UK.** Carol Jarvis is Professor in Knowledge Exchange and Innovation in the Bristol Business School at the University of the West of England. Her research focuses on the application of complexity approaches (Complex Responsive Processes of Relating) to leadership, coaching, innovation, and entrepreneurship, and the everyday experience of change and innovation. She has an active interest in experiential and team-based approaches to learning, from undergraduate students to participants on executive education programmes and played a leading role in designing UWE's suite of team entrepreneurship programmes. Her research is published in *Management Learning*, *Advances in Developing Human Resources*, and *Entrepreneurship Education and Pedagogy*.

**Selen Kars-Unluoglu, Senior Lecturer in Organisation Studies, Bristol Business School, University of West of England, UK.** Selen Kars-Unluoglu is Senior Lecturer in Organisation Studies in the Bristol Business School at the University of West England. She researches the ways organizations and entrepreneurs develop and deploy their intangible resources, such as knowledge, capabilities, and networks to generate growth and achieve learning. Her work is informed interpretative phenomenology and practice-based approaches with a focus on the micro-level and the lived experience. Her attention to the micro-level recently has given rise to a new line of practice-informed inquiry to explore the everyday leaderly practices of ordinary people that redraw the leader-follower relations for the (post)pandemic organizing, which was published in the edited book *Life after Covid: The Other Side of Crisis* (Bristol University Press, 2020). Her research has appeared in *Innovation: Management & Organization, International Small Business Journal,* and *Journal of Management & Organization.*

**Saioa Arando Lasagabaster, Coordinator of People in Cooperation: Leadership and Ownership Research Area, Mondragon University, Spain.** Saioa Arando, PhD, is the coordinator of "People in cooperation: leadership and ownership" research area. She completed her doctorate in Economics at the University of Deusto. In 2006, she was awarded the Vanek-Hovat Prize for best paper by a young economist at the IAFEP International Conference. She is actively collaborating in several research projects with national and international researchers and her work has received funding from different public institutions. Her papers have been published in journals such as *ILR Review, JEBO,* or *Revesco.*

**Karolina Ozadowicz, Team Coach, University of West of England, UK.** Karolina Ozadowicz works as the Team Coach at the University of the West of England. She is currently completing her studies in the Department of Leadership and Organisational Behaviour at the University of Reading. Her background is in professional coaching, mentoring, and social entrepreneurship. She is a Fellow of the Higher Education Academy (AdvanceHE).

**Ann-Cathrin Scheider, Team Coach, University of Applied Sciences Bremerhaven, Germany.** Ann-Cathrin Scheider is a team coach at the Team Academy in Bremerhaven, Germany. She is one of the "co-founders" of this first Team Academy in Germany, which has been initiated by Prof. Michael Vogel 2018. After finishing the Bachelor's Degree in "Cruise Tourism Management", Ann-Cathrin worked as Head of Operations in the UK and Germany, and developed her love for teamwork. During her Master's Degree in "International Business" at the Business School Lausanne, Switzerland, she discovered her interest in education, which she is now using along with her experience coaching leadership teams to foster entrepreneurial competences through the Team Academy model.

**Péter Tasi, Team Coach, University of Applied Sciences Bremerhaven, Germany, and Lecturer, Budapest Business School, Hungary.** Péter Tasi graduated in finance (BA) and in international relations (MA) in Budapest. He started his career as a consultant at an advisory company, dealing with the implementation of EU Funds in the new member state, Hungary. After an "accidental" change to the world of higher education, he discovered the Finnish Team Academy methodology in 2009 and participated in the International Team Mastery 4 Programme. He became one of the founders and was acting as head coach at Team Academy Budapest for 6 years, afterwards gaining a 1-year experience in the UK. Currently, he is a team coach at "Gründung, Innovation, Führung" on the BA Programme in Bremerhaven, Germany. He is also a Lecturer at the Budapest Business School in Hungary.

**Heikki Toivanen, CEO Tiimiakatemia Global Ltd, Finland**. Dr. Heikki Toivanen acts as a team leader (CEO), team coach, team entrepreneur (a partner), and team learner in Tiimiakatemia Global Ltd. Heikki graduated from Aalto University with a master's in mechanical engineering. Heikki's doctoral thesis is about the pulp and paper machinery industrial development in Tampere University of Technology. Heikki started his career as a project manager in Japan for 3 years. He worked over 10 years in leadership and development positions in the pulp and paper machinery company Valmet. Heikki joined Jyväskylä Tiimiakatemia as a team coach in 2008. Heikki became CEO in 2014. Heikki is the author of *Friend Leadership – A Visual Inspiriting Book*.

**Berrbizne Urzelai, Team Coach and Senior Lecturer, University of West of England, UK**. Dr. Berrbizne Urzelai is Team Coach and Senior Lecturer at the University of the West of England (UWE), Bristol, UK. Her teaching and research work is on Strategic Management, International Business, and Entrepreneurship. She holds an international PhD (Hons) in Economics and Business Management (University of Valencia), an MSc in East Asian Studies (University of Bristol), and an MBA (Mondragon University). Her research is related to international business, agglomeration economies, social capital and knowledge management as well as TA-related country and model comparisons. Her research has received several awards (best paper 2017 XXVII ACEDE, best doctoral communication 2015 Torrecid, PhD. Scholarship, etc.).

**Elinor Vettraino, Programme Director and Head Coach, Aston University, UK**. Dr. Elinor Vettraino is Head Coach and Programme Director of the Business Enterprise Development portfolio at Aston University, Birmingham, UK. She also leads the Aston Business Clinic. She is the Founder and Director of Active Imagining, an organizational development and leadership consultancy. She is also a Director of Akatemia UK through which she runs training for academics, consultants, and practitioners who are developing a programme of learning based on the principles of the Team Academy model. Her research is currently based on understanding how the Team Academy model supports transformational learning for participants.

**Amaia Aranceta Zubeldia, Doctoral Student, Faculty of Business, Mondragon University, Spain**. Amaia Aranceta Zubeldia is in her last year of the doctoral program in Social Economy and Advanced Management of Cooperatives in the Faculty of Business of Mondragon Unibertsitatea. She has participated in several forums of social economy, and she has also contributed to several publications like Bilduma edited and published by Mondragon Unibertsitatea. She also did a doctoral stay, successfully completing a course on advanced statistics at the International Summer University in Utrecht (Netherlands) in the year 2018. Apart from her doctoral studies and research program, she works as an English and Social Sciences teacher in a local secondary school.

# Introduction: *Team Academy: Leadership and Teams*

*Elinor Vettraino and Berrbizne Urzelai*

## Team Academy: Philosophy, Pedagogy, Process

Within entrepreneurship education, Team Academy (TA) is seen by some as an innovative pedagogical model that enhances social connectivity as well as experiential (Kayes, 2002; Kolb, 1984), student-centred (Brandes & Ginnis, 1986), and team-based learning (Senge, 1990). It also creates spaces for transformative learning to occur (Mezirow, 1991, 1997, 2008).

*"If you really want to see the future of management education, you should see Team Academy."* Senge (2008) made this comment over a decade ago about TA and since its inception in JAMK – the university of applied sciences, Jyväskylä, Finland in the early 1990s – educators and practitioners engaging in TA-based programmes have continuously pushed at the innovation boundaries of more traditional teaching approaches to education.

TA is often referred to as a model of entrepreneurship education. There are certainly tools, techniques, and approaches that are used within the delivery of a TA-based programme that would support the idea of this being a framework or model that can be applied in different contexts. However, TA is a complex concept appearing not just as a model of activity but also as a pedagogical approach to learning and as a process of self (personal and professional) development. As a pedagogical approach, TA draws on the concept of heutagogical learning (Blaschke & Hase, 2016; Hase & Kenyon, 2001) to develop learners' capacity for self-determination in relation, not just to their academic work but also to their entrepreneurial ventures and their personal and professional development.

Since its creation, the number of institutions adopting this approach has been expanding in many parts of Europe and beyond, and it is increasingly attracting the interest of organizations that want to adopt

DOI: 10.4324/9781003163121-101

a model that emphasizes the transversal competences and skills acquired by its entrepreneurial learners.

## Why This Book Series, and Why Now?

*Berrbizne:*  The idea of publishing a Team Academy (TA) book for me started back in 2017 when I began working in the UK because I could see that there were many differences between how TA was run in Mondragon (Basque Country) and at UWE (UK). In November that year I met with an editor from Routledge and shared some of my ideas which he became excited about. However, it was not until March 2018 that I really started to put some ideas together for the project. I was already in touch with Elinor Vettraino, co-editor of this series, at that time as we were working on several cross-university projects and I remember a conversation I had with her over dinner in Finland in January 2018 (*Tiimiakatemia*'s 25th Anniversary). Essentially, we were discussing why it was that not many people knew about TA even within our institutions. How could it be possible that we were not using the amazing global network more effectively?

*Elinor:*  In June 2018, the Team Academy UK community had their annual meeting event – the TAUK Gathering. During this connection, a number of team coaches met and reflected together about how research could actually inform our team coaching practice, programme design, pedagogical thinking, etc. I was keen to organize a Team Learning Conference where we could invite people from not only TA but also other EE practitioners and academics to present their work and share their knowledge. At this point, Berrbizne and I realized that we had an opportunity to pool our interests together and publish a book for dissemination as well as organize a conference to share knowledge and practice.

*Berrbizne:*  I was about to go on maternity leave, so I thought … this is the moment! I need to do something during this time, so let's work on the book proposal. We created a call for chapters and started reaching out to people from our network to invite them to send us an abstract. The response was great, and we ended up working on a proposal that had too many chapters so Routledge suggested a book series instead. We didn't want to leave people out of this, so we thought *let's do it!* The rest, as they say, is history!

## The Aim of the Series

Surprisingly there is very little published research about the theory and practice behind the Team Academy model so this book series aims to change that position.

We have four main objectives through this project:

- Challenge the existing discourse around entrepreneurship, entrepreneurial activities, and enterprise education, and act as a provocation to generate new knowledge based on team learning and generating networks of teams.
- Collate research, narratives about practice and the experiences of academics, team coaches and team entrepreneurs who have worked with and through the Team Academy model of learning, and to offer new insights to those engaged in developing entrepreneurial education.
- Inspire academics and practitioners to innovate in their delivery methodologies and to explore learning-by-doing approaches to creating value.
- Show the diversity of approaches that exist within the TA network (different institutions, countries, designs, etc.).

We wanted to compile the different research, experiences, and stories about the Team Academy phenomenon throughout its worldwide network. This included not only research but also narrative journeys, reflections, and student voices. This will allow us to get TA on the map when it comes to research as we wanted to show that because you work in TA doesn't mean you can't be a researcher.

There is not a single TA model as different institutions have applied this approach in different ways, so we wanted to celebrate the diversity within the model and create an international network of practitioners and researchers that work around it. This will not only inform our practice but also offer it externally as something to be explored by other educators that is different from traditional learning and teaching models.

## The Story of *Team Academy: Leadership and Teams*

In his 2006 article, Mark Van Vugt posed the view that *"whenever a group of people come together, a leader-follower relationship naturally develops"* (p. 354). The leader-follower relationship in a TA-based education programme can be contentious and challenging, as well as rewarding and enlightening. Learners in these programmes, often situated in Higher Education undergraduate courses, have to work at understanding the psychology and behaviours of those in their teams, and this journey ultimately brings them back to self-reflection.

In this book, the third in the *Routledge Focus on Team Academy* series, researchers and TA practitioners explore the ways in which learners on programmes based on this learning-by-doing model attempt to navigate the complexity of team dynamics while understanding their place and impact on the process. There is often a different approach to leadership taken by TA learners, allowing often for a more fluid and organic emergent process. Self-leadership is a core concept within the model and in this book a number of chapters explore the way in which mindset and understanding of self in teams create opportunities for learning and development that foster entrepreneurial action. The approach to team focuses more on creating communities of practice that can span the global network of programmes inspired by the TA model. In this book, the authors explore the concept of community in teams, and the environment that creates or challenges the Team Entrepreneur (student) as they embark on their entrepreneurial journey. The reader is challenged to consider how such a heutagogical learning model impacts on team identity, performance, and engagement, and how the mental and physical spaces created in such programmes enable the learner to become truly self-determined.

## References

Blaschke, L. M., & Hase, S. (2016). Heutagogy: A holistic framework for creating 21st century self-determined learners. In B. Gros & M. Maina Kinshuk (Eds), *The future of ubiquitous learning: Learning designs for emerging pedagogies* (pp. 25–40). NYC: Springer.

Brandes, D., & P. Ginnis (1986). *A guide to student centred learning.* Oxford: Blackwell.

Hase, S., & Kenyon, C. (2001). Moving from andragogy to heutagogy: Implications for VET. In *Proceedings of research to reality: Putting VET research to work: Australian Vocational Education and Training Research Association (AVETRA)*, Adelaide, SA, 28–30 March. NSW: AVETRA, Crows Nest.

Kayes, D. C. (2002). Experiential learning and its critics: Preserving the role of experience in management learning and education. *Academy of Management Learning & Education, 1*(2), 137–149. doi:10.5465/amle.2002.8509336

Kolb, D. A. (1984) *Experiential learning: Experience as the source of learning and development*. Englewood Cliffs, NJ: Prentice-Hall, Inc.

Mezirow, J. (1991). *Transformative dimensions of adult learning*. San Francisco: Jossey-Bass.

Mezirow, J. (1997). Transformative learning: Theory to practice. In P. Cranton (Ed.), *Transformative learning in action. Vol. 74: New directions for adult and continuing education* (pp. 5–12). San Francisco: Jossey-Bass.

Mezirow, J. (2008). An overview on transformative learning. In K. Illeris (Ed.), *Contemporary theories of learning: Learning theorists in their own words* (pp. 90–105). London: Routledge.

Senge, P. (1990). *Fifth discipline: The art and practice of the learning organisation*. London: Century.

Senge, P. (2008). Peter Senge - Team Academy. Tiimiakatemia Global Ltd, YouTube Channel.

Van Vugt, M. (2006). Evolutionary origins of leadership and followership. *Personality and Social Psychology Review*, *10*(4), 354–371. doi:10.1207/s15327957pspr1004_5

# 1 Understanding Team Performance Indicators in Team Academy

*Marcellin Grandjean and Colin Dargent*

## Introduction

What does it mean to have a high-performing team in a Team Academy (TA)? The intention of our chapter is to share our thoughts on the performance indicators of a team of students following a TA course. We make assumptions based on our experience. We hope that our chapter inspires readers to reflect on the impact of team dynamics on performance in learning contexts.

The team is a central component of the TA approach and its main point of differentiation from other degree-level programmes. For students, having to work in a team with "strangers" who are between 18 and 25 years old is not an easy thing to do as it is often the first group experience for them. The question of success and performance is at the heart of the challenge and is often a source of tension.

In a business context, performance is closely linked to profitability, the main objective of the company. The development of the individual is secondary, although it is increasingly taken into consideration. Valérie Brunel, a French doctor in sociology and psychosociology, talks about this in her book *Les managers de l'âme*. In the programmes based on the TA approach, it is the other way round, the development of the individual is the primary objective and profitability, we will talk more about turnover in these programmes, which is a means to this end. Thus, we have focused this study around the following two questions: What is a learning AND performing team? Do productivity-focused team models apply to TA teams?

To answer these questions, we took as our subject of study a team that is part of the Bachelor Team Entrepreneur (BTE) course at the

DOI: 10.4324/9781003163121-1

University of Strasbourg's School of Management. Created in 2011, this course is based on the TA approach. Teamwork is at the heart of the BTE. From the beginning of the students' time on the course, each of them joins a team for the three years of the course and participates in collective half-day coaching sessions twice a week to learn through exchange with the other members around the projects and readings in progress.

Twice a year, the programme organizes Learning Sets – a community event involving all BTE teams where students present a paper on a topic of their choice based on their experience and reading. Teamwork topics are among the most popular. Theoretical models from the business world such as Katzenbach and Smith (1992), Drexler and Sibbet (1966), or Tuckman (1965) are often cited and a debate is launched on the relevance of applying these models in the BTE context.

This chapter is a reflective piece of work presented at Learning Sets on the subject of team performance in TA. The study was conducted by Marcellin Grandjean and Colin Dargent, respectively, coach and member of the team studied during Colin's third year of study.

Firstly, we present the history of Colin's team's three years of study at BTE. Secondly, we analyse the evolution of Colin's team over these three years using the models of Katzenbach and Smith (1992) and Tuckman (1965). These two models describe the evolution of a team through different stages. After a brief reminder of these stages, we will compare them to the experience of the team studied.

The testimonies collected during the study led to several questions which we have tried to answer in the last part of this chapter.

## The Story of a Student Team at TA

To map the history of the team, we organized a workshop in which all team members participated to share their experiences from the time they joined the BTE in September 2016 until April 2019. The students identified the key moments that marked the changes in the team's dynamics, which helped to define the periods. For each period, the students had to imagine writing a chapter of a book and characterize it with a title, the main events, the feelings of the team members, and the energy level. This data was supplemented by individual interviews and feedback from the coaches on the nature of the coaching adopted in the period concerned.

## First Year

Period 1: Discovery
   Energy level: 7/10

**Main events**

4 September 2016

The 24 new students join the course. They attend the BTE presentation day and participate in the integration weekend organized for the whole community (students and coaches).

Following a test by Belbin (2010), the students are divided into two teams of 12. On the whole, everyone is happy with their teammates. The first objective of the year set by the coach is to make a turnover that will finance the participation of each member in the start-up weekend. It is an entrepreneurial event that takes place over a weekend with the objective of proposing project ideas, forming a team and presenting a prototype to a jury at the end.

October–December 2016

To reach the goal, the two teams adopt the strategy of "small projects" for example setting up bun sales, holding a stand at the Management School to sell pancakes and sandwiches or market studies for clients.

**Dominant feelings:** Positive dynamics, uneven level of action, creation of the first clans, motivated, euphoria, fear

**Student voices:**

> *"I was out of the sessions, I wasn't talking, I didn't understand what was going on"*

> *"I was super excited and lost at the same time"*

**Nature of coaching:** The role of the coach is to lay the foundations for dialogue. He stimulates action and takes the lead in the sessions.

Period 2: The flame
Energy level: 6/10

**Main events**

January 2017–April 2017

The next objective set by the coach is to finance a team trip in May. The first conflicts start to appear. The topics concern investment in long- or short-term projects, managing money together or individually. At the same time, team projects emerge such as the realization of the 24-hour customer service.

**Dominant feelings:** under pressure, cohesion to achieve goals, early successes

**Student voices:**

> *"It's a war in the team – if you don't do CA, you're not going to leave. There's tension".*
>
> *"I felt part of a team".*

**Nature of coaching:** Cohesion seems to be the key word in the coaching strategy. The coach has a facilitating role in group coaching sessions.

---

Period 3: The adventures
Energy level: 2/10

**Main events**

May 2017– June 2017

Back from the trip, everyone was able to learn a lot more about their teammates. End-of-year assessments are approaching, time to fill in the portfolios. The commitment to action in the teams drops. Several students announce their departure from the course.

**Dominant feelings:** Reality check, stress, misunderstanding, questioning, being left out, absences

**Student voices:**

> *"We came back from Finland, we almost all hated each other"*

> *"all year the coaches have been advocating team building and dialogue… and now they make a decision without dialogue with us"*

**Nature of coaching:** After a number of student departures and a long reflection, the coaches decided to merge the two teams and make one team of 16 members.

---

### Second Year

Period 4: The desert
Energy level: 1/10

**Main events**

September 2017–March 2018

New team, new coach, new goals … In short, a new start. We can distinguish two states of mind among the students: the sceptics and the optimists. The commitment to the overall team action is very low. Absences, lateness, and non-compliance with commitments are the daily routine of this group.

**Dominant feelings:** Loss of trust, uneasiness, unspoken words, lack of motivation, no cohesion, new clans are created.

**Student voices:**

> *"I realise that I cannot trust the team"*

> *"My energy was very, very low. No direction, no motivation"*.

**Nature of coaching:** Coaching is very much about the team and achieving a common project. Individual projects are side-lined with the introduction of in and out projects. A project is considered "in" if the turnover generated by the project goes to the team account. If this is not the case, the project is considered "out". The learning and turnover achieved in these projects will not be taken into account in the evaluation or the objectives. Tensions emerge between some students and the coach.

Period 4: The Mirage
Energy level: 2/10

**Main events**

March 2018–April 2018

At the beginning of the year, the coaches had insisted on the importance of having a common project, which brings together the whole team or at least a majority of its members. But this initiative was a failure and generated conflict. The trust between the coach and the team is very low. The approach to evaluations only worsens the dynamic. On the action side, it is again quite disparate. While some people launch projects and start to make turnover, others do not manage to get past this stage, which creates a rift in the team.

**Dominant feelings:** Letting go, letting go, disengagement, hypocrisy

**Student voices:**

> "*I was doing my own thing, working alone, not paying too much attention to what was going on in the session*"

> "*We were trying to find solutions that work for everyone*".

**Nature of coaching:** After a brief withdrawal of the coach and a partial resolution of the conflicts, things return to normal.

---

Period 5: Back to reality
Energy level: 3/10

**Main events**

May 2018–August 2018

Assessment period. Some people realize that it is going to be difficult to meet the expectations. Some have cheated by copying and pasting. We learned during the summer that some will miss their year. The holidays are coming and there are new departures in the team following the evaluations.

**Dominant feelings:** happy that some are leaving, lassitude, shock of evaluations.

**Student voices:**

> *"I didn't see it coming, and at the assessments the axe falls!"*
>
> *"I was waiting for the end of the year, for some people to leave".*

**Nature of coaching:** Coaching focused on compliance with the evaluation framework.

---

**Third Year**

Period 6: Renewal, blossoming
Energy level: 5/10

**Main events**

September 2018–January 2019

Once again, the team undergoes a significant change in membership. After 5 departures and 2 arrivals (last year's repeaters), the team has 13 members. Marcellin became the new coach of the team. The dynamic is however different from the one at the beginning of the second year. Everyone, marked by a trying second year, adopts a more individualistic posture. The training sessions are relaxed and the commitment to action is much more uniform than in previous years. The team still has two departures which will not really have an impact on its dynamics.

**Dominant feelings:** Acceptance, wisdom, caution, respect, tolerance, experience
**Nature of coaching:** The coach is much more present in TS and also brings content. The coach has a supporting role.

---

To summarize all this data, we have created a summary diagram (Figure 1.1).
We will now understand the dynamics of this team through the team development models of Katzenbach and Smith (1992) and Tuckman (1965).

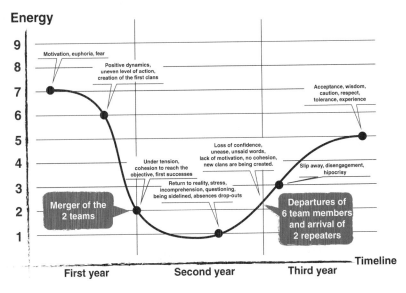

**Energy**

*Figure 1.1* The journey of the team throughout the BTE programme.

Source: Authors' own.

## The Katzenbach and Smith (1992) Model

We define a team as a group of people with complementary skills who are committed to a common goal and approach for which they are mutually responsible. The different levels of team have been defined by Katzenbach and Smith (1992) as ranging from a working group to a high-performance team:

- Working group: The group members meet to share information, but so far there are no common objectives that require mutual accountability. Each team member is solely responsible for the work delegated to him/her by the group.
- Pseudo-team: This level is at the bottom of the performance curve. The group functions like a team but is not a team. The members do not yet dare to commit themselves. Not everyone takes responsibility for the common goal.
- Potential team: At this stage, the team members converge on a common goal and a path to get there. They work more efficiently, and everyone takes responsibility.

- Real team: At this level, the team has a clearly defined common approach and goal. Their skills are complementary, and they take responsibility for their results, both positive and negative.
- High-performance team: The difference between a real team and a successful team lies in the relationships between the team members. Performance is the result of team members being mutually committed to the development of individuals and the team.

Let's compare our data, the team's experience described in the first part, with Katzenbach and Smith's (1992) stages.

It is important to note that the study team underwent significant changes in membership at the beginning of each year. In retrospect, there was not one but three teams, with a new team being formed at the beginning of each study year. As a result, the students started each new year at the working group stage. In the first year, the study team was indeed a small group with skills and was committed to an objective with performance goals. However, the collective did not have a common approach and the students did not feel mutually accountable. In the second year, as the results show, the group was still at the pseudo-team stage. Finally, they never went beyond the stage of a potential team, a level that the team reached in the first and third years.

## Tuckman's (1965) Model

Bruce Tuckman published his model on team dynamics in 1965. It consists of four stages: forming, storming, norming, and performing. It is a cycle that the team will go through over a longer or shorter period of time. Moreover, the evolution of a team is not a linear thing. A team in norming can easily go back to the storming phase.

Let's start by briefly recalling what these four phases correspond to.

- Forming: At this stage, we cannot yet speak of a team but more of a group of people. There are no common objectives yet and the different members are getting to know each other.
- Storming: As the name suggests, this phase can be the "trickiest" for a team to go through. Several postures emerge. While some will try to impose their ideas, others will, on the contrary, completely step aside. A common objective emerges but opinions differ on how to achieve it. This is surely the stage where the team is least productive from an economic point of view.

- Norming: Team members begin to know each other better. Conflicts and debates give way to action and cooperation. Common values and rules of conduct begin to emerge within the group. This stage marks the beginning of cohesion within the group.
- Performing: This is the stage where the *I* becomes *we*. The team members work together effectively to achieve the common goal. Responsibility is shared and everyone knows their role.

For the team studied, there was not one but three teams, one per year. In the first and third years, the team reached the norming stage. In the second year, the team remained stuck in the storming phase. What is interesting to note is that the collective in the third year, marked by a difficult second year, did not really experience a storming phase.

It should also be noted that in a BTE team, turnover is only a means to an end, which is learning. And from this point of view, the storming phase is surely the richest of the four, even though it is the least efficient phase from the point of view of profitability.

## What Is a Successful Team in TA-Based Training?

With these team development models in mind, the coaches have, from the beginning of the coaching, focused on the team and the desire to create a high-performance team.

Feedback from students when they were in the first and second years, where the coaching focus was more on the team:

> *"Coach's attempt to propose team projects ... We just had a fight and we are asked to work together: 'it's dead'".*

> *"In the first year the coach followed up on the team trip "where are you now? The coach facilitated several team visioning workshops".*

It is observed that students have an idealized view of the team, which prevents team members from seeing themselves as such. This makes the achievement of this state of performance unattainable for everyone. We can understand the complexity of achieving high performance with the student feedback below:

> *"we are not a team"*

> *"I can't trust others"*

> *"we are not performing well"*

In the third year, with this in mind, the coaches changed their focus to be more student-centred, and again feedback from the students echoes this:

> "*Change of coaching in the third year, more in the accomplishment of each one*"

We observe that the change in team dynamics occurred when the focus of the coaches shifted from the team to the individual and, at the same time, the students accepted each other and their team situation.

> "*not necessarily joint action, but common individual objectives (future, graduation ...)*"

> "*healthy atmosphere. No nit-picking. Acceptance of lateness and behaviour*"

> "*When I leave the team due to illness, I have even more courriel to come back to the team. Supported when another student asks me to do activities with him/her (important act: an attention to the absent)*"

The change of perspective on team performance allows us to approach certain phases of team development differently. Thus, we can ask ourselves, what exactly does it mean to be a high-performing team in the context of a training course such as the BTE?

In a business context, the focus is on productivity, the development of the individual is secondary. At BTE, it is the other way around, the development of the individual is the primary objective and productivity is a means to that end. Shouldn't coaches focus on individual performance supported by the team rather than team performance supported by each individual? Bearing in mind that the primary aim of the BJE is individual learning and development, a successful team would be one that provides a supportive framework for each member to experiment and develop their own skills. Thus, the storming phase, which from a productive team perspective is the most difficult phase, becomes the most learning phase and the one where the individual develops the most. In this respect, it is worth noting that the focus on the individual at this stage can enable students to see the team as a strength, rather than a liability. The norming and then performing phases would be the ones where the individual is recognized and aware of the learning they have had and the learning they are developing. The team spirit and the team's performance stem from this.

The change in the performance indicator implies a questioning of the team development models where performance is associated with economic profitability. We believe that the team's performance would be limited by the beliefs constructed in the non-commitment phase. In the team studied, the non-commitment phase lasted 1 year, and the sum of the beliefs became important and disabling.

Finally, what would the team development model be if the focus was on individual performance supported by the team and not the team supported by the individual? Two curves emerge. The first shown in Figure 1.2 focuses on the performance of the team, with a lower start in terms of performance than what can be found on the Katzenbach and Smith (1992) performance curve, a shorter low non-commitment phase and a higher performance potential.

Thanks to this new perspective, we believe that the non-commitment phase will be shorter, the number of beliefs about the team created is lower, and the performance of the team is therefore more important.

The second curve, which is emerging, represents the amount of personal development of individuals in the team. It would be low at the beginning, with a strong growth in the non-engagement phase, and then a slow progression in the team performance phase (Figure 1.3).

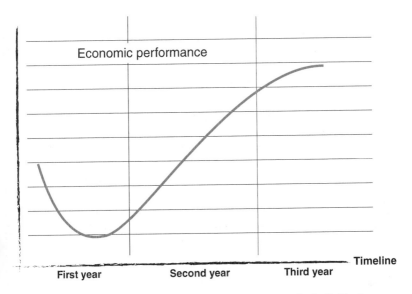

*Figure 1.2* Performance of the team if the focus was on the individual.
Source: Authors' own.

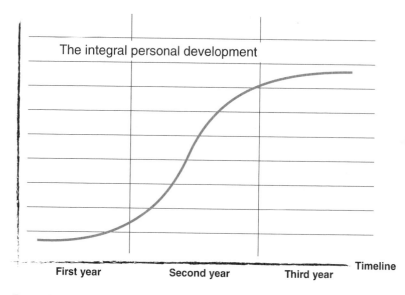

*Figure 1.3* Personal development of team members.
Source: Authors' own.

The sharing of this study was a high point in the BTE community following which the coaches modified the pedagogical framework of the training by introducing individual coaching, which until then had not been very present in the training. The collective coaching strategy has also been reviewed with a greater emphasis on the development of each individual.

In the following year, the two new teams also experienced significant departures. Even though the teams contained few members, the coaches looked for other solutions than merging the teams, even if from a financial point of view the constraint remained important. For example, one of the training sessions was done jointly but the identities of the teams remained intact for these teams, the storming phases lasted less time and there were fewer team departures at the end of the second year. One of the teams was even a refuge for two members of the team studied here, where they could be welcomed and recognized.

## Conclusion

Our conclusion is that the classic team development model cannot be applied to BTE teams because the performance indicator is not the same. In a team whose purpose is productivity, it is the individual who serves the group. Conversely, in a team whose purpose is the personal development of its members, it is the team that serves the individuals. The question we now ask ourselves is: What would be the economic performance of a team that focuses on the development of the skills of the individual?

## References

Belbin, R. M. (2010). *Team roles at work*. London: Routledge.

Brunel, V. (2008). *Les managers de l'âme: Le developpement personnel en enterprise, nouvelle pratique de pouvoir?* France: Le Découverte/Poche.

Drexler, A., & Sibbet, D. (1966). Team performance model. www.davidsibbet.com/process-models/

Katzenbach, J. R., & Smith, D. K. (1992). *The wisdom of teams: Creating the high performance organization*. Harvard, MA: Harvard Business Review Press.

Tuckman, B. W. (1965). *Developmental sequence in small groups*. Washington DC: American Psychological Association.

# 2 Team Companies as Communities of Practice: Considerations and Reflections for Future Practice

*Berrbizne Urzelai*

## Facilitating Communities of Practice

Learning processes are intrinsically social and collective and occur not only through imitation but because of joint contributions to the understanding of complex problems, or when people are brought together to share experiences and past stories (Teece et al., 1997). Socialization is crucial for knowledge creation (Nonaka & Takeuchi, 1995). This goes in line with Healey et al. (2016), who emphasized the importance of creating learning communities that help to foster engagement and to create a transformative learning experience. Entrepreneurial learning is not just an individual process; various researchers have demonstrated it is social and it has important networking aspects (Lockett et al., 2017; Pittaway & Thorpe, 2012; Wang & Chugh, 2014).

Communities of practice (CoPs) are defined as *"groups of people who share a concern, a set of problems, or a passion about a topic, and who deepen their knowledge and expertise in this area by interacting on an ongoing basis"* (Wenger et al., 2002, p. 7). Members are held together by a common interest in a body of knowledge and are driven by a desire and need to share problems, experiences, insights, templates, tools, and best practices (Hubert et al., 2001). The purpose of a CoP is to create, expand, and exchange knowledge, and to develop individual skills for a professional practice (Moingeon et al., 2006, p. 12).

The *CoP* provides a perspective to complement the commonly action-oriented individual-centred perspective on entrepreneurial learning (Pittaway & Cope, 2007). These communities are usually described through three dimensions: the domain, the community, and the practice, and they can adopt different forms. To explain it simply, we have a community of people that care about a domain of knowledge, with a defined set of issues. In order to be effective in their

DOI: 10.4324/9781003163121-2

domain, they share practice, which includes frameworks, ideas, tools, information, styles, languages, stories, and documents. These dimensions adapt and change while the community evolves and develops through different stages (potential, coalescing, maturing, stewardship, and transformation stages) as the level of energy and visibility that the community generates changes over time. A *CoP* can adopt different forms in terms of its size, durability, heterogeneity, boundaries, or motives for its creation (Wenger et al., 2002).

The members of the *CoP* do not necessarily work together every day, but they meet because they find value in their interactions, i.e. learning together, accumulating knowledge, and becoming informally bound (Wenger et al., 2002). This value is not just instrumental for their work as it also accrues in the personal satisfaction of knowing people that understand each other's perspective and of belonging to an interesting group of people. This value can also adopt the form of sharing information, insights, and advice; helping to solve problems; discussing their situations, their aspirations, and their needs; exploring new ideas; and acting as sounding boards. According to those authors, the value of the *CoP* can be classified into short-term or long-term value, and into whether the benefits are mainly for the individual members (i.e. improve the experience of work, foster professional development) or the organization as a whole (i.e. improve business outcomes, develop organizational capabilities). Other authors (Allee, 2000; Chu et al., 2012) suggest that beyond the individual (help people be efficient, sense of safety, etc.) or the enterprise (solve problems, drive strategy, recruit talent, opportunities for innovation, etc.), there are benefits for the community too (spread knowledge and expertise, power sharing and influence, etc.).

Interestingly, Roberts (2006) argues that in the USA or the UK, where the pursuit of neo-liberalism with its emphasis on the market and the individual has eroded the sense of community over more than 25 years, *CoPs* may be a less effective means through which to organize knowledge creation and transfer.

As Wenger et al. (2002) explain, there are different degrees of community of practice participation: peripheral (observants who rarely participate, and focus on superficial practice development tasks), active (attending regular meetings but without intensity), or core group (sharing know-how, developing knowledge, taking on community projects, driving the *CoP*, etc.) members. Borzillo et al. (2011), for instance, define a process (awareness, allocation, accountability, architectural, and advertising) where members can move from the periphery to the core.

The most important factor in a community's success is the vitality of its leadership. The community coordinator is a respected, knowledgeable, connected, and passionate community member who helps the community focus on its domain, maintain relationships, and develop its practice by recognizing the development needs of the members (Wenger et al., 2002). They can perform functions such as assessing the health of the community and evaluate its contribution or identify issues in their domain. Garavan et al. (2007) studied the strategies and processes used by *CoP* managers when managing intentionally created *CoPs* and they found the following ones:

1 Negotiating meaning: building a collective understanding of what the CoP is about.
2 Learning by doing: learning from mistakes, talking, and listening.
3 Interpreting the situation and context: enabling members to interpret it and not impose a specific understanding or view.
4 Articulating vision, goals, objectives, and activities: translate general statement of purpose into specific objectives and tasks (balance the big and small picture).
5 Unearthing and challenging assumptions and beliefs on action: bring different views together.
6 Building shared meaning: articulate where the CoP is going, its purpose and terms of reference.
7 Preparing the CoP report: use shared artefacts and resources as a medium of communication, stimulus for discussion, and catalyst for collaboration.
8 Building trust and enabling collaboration: integration and networking skills.
9 Identification of individual CoP members' skills, talents, and knowledge
10 Creating synergies within the CoP: careful facilitation and articulation of expectations.
11 Developing relational resources: interpersonal strategies stimulating questions, seeking reactions, encouraging debate, acting as a moderator, setting agendas, and seeking closure.
12 Focus on intrinsic motivation: knowing the members and understanding their motivations.
13 Setting challenges for individuals: share the vision in an inspirational way and frame the priorities in a way they motivate members.
14 Balancing constraints and freedoms: know when to exert pressure and let the members breathe.

15 Managing the power dynamics: encourage members to build on others' contributions.
16 Setting the rules: setting the agenda and rules (timing of meetings, commitment, prep work, etc.).
17 Managing conflicts: reinspire and get members moving again.
18 Managing boundaries: provide space for fun but set limits of the playground.
19 Coach and role model: use coaching techniques to develop cohesiveness, contribute to the atmosphere of the team, and manage conflict issues.
20 Face-to-face meetings and personal relationships: to build teamwork and manage power.

## Team Coaching

There is no clear definition of what team coaching is in the literature. Clutterbuck (2011) describes the competencies of coaches for each of the three levels of a coaching dialogue. For level 1, for instance, this would include listening skills, observing and assessing performance, giving feedback, motivating people to pursue their goals, encouraging people to support each other in learning, social, technical, tactical, and strategic dialogue, or demonstrating good practice. Woodhead (2019) argues that there are some particular attributes of team coaching that may enhance team working by, for instance, providing a forum for dialogue, giving focus and clarity for shared goals, increasing trust and collaboration, enabling a systemic understanding to problem solving, decisions-making, and commitment to achieving collective outcomes, helping to develop personal and interpersonal relationships, or creating a sense of belonging and an understanding of each other.

If we look at the Team Academy (TA) programme at UWE, Team Entrepreneurship, *team coaches* support student teams and individuals through their educational pathway as well as the practical concept development (Davey, 2017, p. 5). TA literature describes the central points of team coaching in the *theses of team coaching* (Partanen, 2012, p. 110). These state that team coaching can be learned through several years of experience and a learning network of team coaches and that the coach's personality is the most important tool. They also emphasize the importance of dialogue (key in the process), conflicts (as opportunities of learning), and diversity (as a resource), and how together with the team, the team coach creates an atmosphere of trust. Also described are the qualities of a team coach, which include, among others, creativity, the ability to find new solutions, being real, or being aware of one's own feelings and goals. These considerations are important when we evaluate the role of the team coach within TA and as a CoP manager.

## Methodology

In terms of the research context, in Finland, *team companies* (TCs) are legal entities (co-ops) and they pay corporate taxes but are totally owned by the teampreneurs (Davey, 2017). They can also serve as incubators, as new product and service innovations created within TA have frequently led to students continuing as independent entrepreneurs in new businesses after graduating. This is different in the UK as they do not necessarily create legal entities, but still work as learning organizations (Senge, 1990).

The social constructivism approach focuses on active learning within groups, where individuals form and construct knowledge by assigning personal meaning to it (Akinoglu & Yasar, 2007). This philosophy resonates well with my personal interest on analysing the details of a situation to reflect from that and motivate actions on the workplace and my coaching practice.

The study then adopts a case study research strategy (Saunders et al., 2015) and more specifically a single embedded case study (Yin, 2009) that attempts to gain a deep understanding of the Why's and How's of a phenomenon, in this case, the functioning of the TC as a CoP. As Flyvbjerg (2006) argues, a case study could illuminate the general by looking at the particular and serve as a force of example.

The research adopts an action research approach. Eden and Huxham (1996, p. 75) argue that the findings of action research result from *"involvement with members of an organization over a matter which is of genuine concern to them"*. The researcher is part of the organization within which the research and the change process are taking place (Coghlan & Brannick, 2005). In this case, the researcher (me) is at the same time the team coach of the TC. This pedagogical research approach allows the exploration of the students' experience of learning at the same time as giving me the opportunity to reflect on my practice. Therefore, the findings will also include personal reflections and observations about my team coaching practice.

For data collection, primary of a qualitative nature, documentary data and semi-structured interviews were used. The documentary data was based on the feedback that all the 18 TC members gave me in June 2018. The interviews were conducted between July and November 2018 and four team members were selected for this. The selection criterion was their engagement level in year 1 (more than 75% of attendance) and the diversity in academic performance, measured by their average marks at year 1.

Ferguson et al. (2004, p. 54) argue that ethical issues arise from the fiduciary relationship between faculty and their students, and violations of that relationship occur when the educator has a dual role (double agency) as a researcher with those students. This conflict is particularly evident in faculty research on pedagogy in their own disciplines, for which students are necessary as participants but are captive in the relationship. This is a research limitation within this study, but I made it clear that I was acting as a researcher rather than a team coach for the purpose of this project.

We need to consider that this research is just base on a case study/ TC, which has limitations in terms of generalizing its results. The purpose however is not to produce a theory that is generalizable to all populations but to explain what is going on in that particular research setting, so as to make me reflect about my team coaching practice through research.

## Findings

Through the research process, I could explore to what extent the TC was behaving as a learning community, which made me think about certain elements of my practice. In this section, I will present some of the findings of the analysis along with my personal reflection as a team coach of that team.

### *The TC as a Community of Practice*

The findings show that there is a generalized agreement that the TC could be considered a CoP for the descriptors and elements that define the concept (Figure 2.1). The students have defined it as a small, short-lived, co-located, heterogeneous, internal, and intentional CoP where the domains are related to *"being an entrepreneur and having a positive impact in the environment"* (Wenger et al., 2002). However, one thing that was quite evident was that the concept of enterprise entrepreneurship is complex and not all the members have exactly the same understanding of what being an entrepreneur is (some link it to venture creation, some to the acquisition of enterprising competencies, etc.).

However, there are different views about the concept and *value of the CoP* and the engagement of its members. While some with

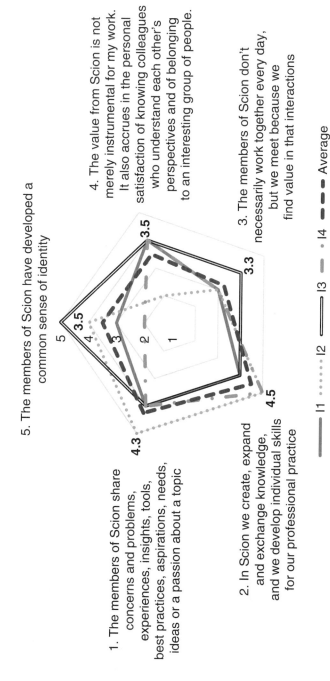

5. The members of Scion have developed a common sense of identity

4. The value from Scion is not merely instrumental for my work. It also accrues in the personal satisfaction of knowing colleagues who understand each other's perspectives and of belonging to an interesting group of people.

3. The members of Scion don't necessarily work together every day, but we meet because we find value in that interactions

1. The members of Scion share concerns and problems, experiences, insights, tools, best practices, aspirations, needs, ideas or a passion about a topic

2. In Scion we create, expand and exchange knowledge, and we develop individual skills for our professional practice

I1 ········ I2 ——— I3 ——— I4 ━ ━ Average

*Figure 2.1* The TC as a learning CoP.
Source: Author's own.

leadership roles in the TC emphasize how the community brings value to their business projects, leadership, and decision-making processes, others believe that the team is composed of individuals with different ideas and no *common sense of identity*.

> *"I have specially learnt about leadership and how to work with others. You get support for everything, and you improve the quality of making decisions. In this environment we increase our employ-ability and we get things that we would not get from a mainstream course. However, I am not sure if everyone is totally aware of what our practice or our values are".* (I1)

> *"We do find a value in our interaction (social, doing our assignments together, etc.) but there are different groups within the team and some people work on their own and do not really interact with team members that much. Certain members may have more instrumental reasons and do not know the purpose of the team but a lot of us share a common sense of identity".* (I2)

> *"A lot of members meet in the hub to work on projects or assignments, but not everyone. However, it is true that we always talk about the team to others and we are happy and proud to be on it. I am not 100% about the sense of belonging and commitment as some members lack motivation or have personal issues going on ... sometimes it's difficult with such a big group".* (I3)

> *"We are a team but we are all very individual. Everyone feels they belong to the team but everyone has different ideas on what the team is".* (I4)

This shows there are sub-groups within the team and that, as we described in the literature, the level of participation within the community could be different. Some members are more active or in the core, while others are more peripheral. Although the TC has developed a team strategy (common goals, a mission, vision and values, KPIs, etc.), not all members seem to be following this strategy. By what I have seen in this programme and probably due to cultural reasons, the TCs in the UK adopt a much more individualistic approach. I took those findings as an opportunity to identify those more disengaged groups and work with the two team leaders to motivate those members to work towards the agreed future strategic pathway of the team. I arranged 1 to 1 meetings to follow up on their goals and give them feedback. It was a good moment for the team to realize how their individual and team goals should be aligned.

The team identifies its *practice* as related to having shared standards, rules, tools, principles, or shared communication channels.

> *"We have training sessions to share knowledge, things like pre and post project reviews, learning contracts to understand people further, ground rules, a balanced scorecard, project feedback sessions and a project database".* (I1)

> *"We share documents and reports in a shared space. We also have shared standards and team rules and we know what we can expect from the team".* (I2)

> *"We have ground rules to keep everything into place, be focused and know what is expected in the training sessions, we use Pebble Pad, project reports, and google docs to document the learning and experiences and keep that information, and we communicate through Team Reach, social media and emails".* (I3)

It seems that for them, the *social element of not only the team but also the whole TE community* is very important in order to improve their performance as a team, develop trust, and therefore, share knowledge, but there are different views on how much this social element has been cultivated.

> *"We have a lot of socials and we are building mutual commitment. Everyone is getting to know each other better and finding out what drives and motivates people".* (I2)

> *"Not everyone shares their learning in the team. The effort and time have not been put into making Scion more of a team by bonding outside training sessions. It could have potential but it is not as good as it could be".* (I3)

As a team coach, I tried to engage with them outside the training sessions by going to social events (i.e. escape room, Christmas dinner). It is important for the coach to support this, as building rapport is crucial for a good coaching relationship (Boyce et al., 2010; Brown & Grant, 2010). There is an acknowledgement in the team that they are gaining common *trust*, improving mutual accountability and support, but there is potential for more learning from crystalizing their reflections and conducting more team projects.

> *"We are getting better at sharing everything which is in line with our value of transparency. You can get good advice from members and*

*that helps you create best practices. We can share and exchange more knowledge but we need to put a proper system so that everyone does it. We need to improve the social creation of knowledge. Conflict as a source of learning is something we are trying to use now as we have not always spoken the truth or ask hard questions".* (I1)

*"We are very much a learning sort of team. We are getting so much better to provide advice and feedback but as a team we could work better in the more tangible things of creating reports, etc. The team is a group of people I can trust, it's a safe space. People think we are a strong team because we have so many individual projects but we don't really have many team projects. We are missing value from not doing that".* (I2)

*"We have a safe space to share our experiences, but I would not say the CoP have an effect on me and performance as an entrepreneur. When we do research undertakings we could combine the knowledge to assist us on creating better project reports and reflections".* (I3)

This drove several conversations with the team leaders and the dialogue sessions with the team, they decided to *structure their learning* by focusing on projects and ventures on Tuesdays and on academic-related aspects on Thursdays to balance the time they were allocating to share and create this knowledge.

### The Team Coach's Role

Within HE, I often feel that I have to choose between doing research or teaching, or coaching and teaching, but *"the time has come to move beyond the tired old 'teaching versus research' debate and give the familiar and honorable term 'scholarship' a broader, more capacious meaning, one that brings legitimacy to the full scope of academic work"* (Boyer, 1990, p. 16). Thus, this section will reflect on the educator perspective, in this case, my role as a team coach as a way to progress in my knowledge on Scholarship of Teaching and Learning of Entrepreneurship Education.

Through this research, I had the chance to reflect on my role as a team coach (Clutterbuck, 2011) and my role as a CoP manager (Garavan et al., 2007). By studying these two concepts, I found a lot of similarities among them. The following tables show some of the answers given by the students, which in a sense confirms that I am using the tools I have in hand to perform as a team coach, and sometimes I am adopting the role of a CoP manager within my academic practice and my learning relationship with them (Tables 2.1 and 2.2).

*Table 2.1* The role of the team coach

| The Role of the Team Coach | Examples Given by Students (The Coach Does This …) |
| --- | --- |
| Listening skills | During training sessions (I1) |
| | This link with the next 2, observing and giving feedback too. She listens to what the team says and evaluates from what we say, what we actually do and achieve or not (I2). |
| | Through a lot of feedback that we are given about how to improve the training sessions. She listens, take things on board (I3) |
| | She knows all what is going on in the team (I4) |
| Observing and assessing performance | During training sessions and outside training sessions with academic work (I1) |
| | From listening us from in the 1 to 1s she then has been giving feedback, then after observing training session she gives constructive feedback to training session leaders (I3) |
| | By giving feedback (I4) |
| Giving feedback | With 1 to 1 meetings (I1) |
| | The feedback she gives on project Tuesdays (I4) |
| Motivate people to pursue their goals | When she reminds us about our learning contract goals (I1) |
| | Not 100% on goals but she does with projects and assignments. She shares information and knowledge. Knowing there is someone that supports motivates people to improve (I3). |
| | This is more done by the team members, seeing each other presenting projects on Tuesdays (I4) |
| | You increased my motivation by giving constructive feedback and advice (documentary analysis). |
| Encourage people to support each other in learning | During training sessions (I1) |
| | By setting an example on showing how to support each other in academic and project work encourages people (I3) |
| | This falls more into the team. If we want to help each other it happens (I4) |
| Social, technical, tactical, and strategic dialogue | By making sure team members are ok welfare-wise and during discussions about our mission, vision, values and ground rules (I1) |
| | Yes quite often we have talks when we get stuck and the coach suggests why *don't you think about this?*. She has also taken care for example that the Finish girls integrate socially (I4) |

*(Continued)*

*Table 2.1* (Continued)

| The Role of the Team Coach | Examples Given by Students (The Coach Does This ...) |
| --- | --- |
| Demonstrating good practice | Not giving up when Scion as a team is stubborn, by showing them good practices (I3).<br>She brings best practices on ground rules for example and then the team decides what to do with that. She is very good at bringing to us what other team academies do (I4) |

Source: Author's own.

It became quite apparent that the 1 to 1 meetings with the team-preneurs were highly valuable to the team and that the team members (not the team coach or not only the team coach) play a crucial role in some of those elements (i.e. motivation, setting up rules).

Although Partanen's laws indicate, *"the team coach is not a member of the team. You are a friend, but you are not a friend"* (Partanen, 2012, p. 111) the students sometimes saw the team coach as *a team member.* This is interesting, as it shows how much we work in partnership for their learning, as they do not see me as an authority figure or someone that tells them what to do. Their feedback shows the high level of autonomy and responsibility that they are adopting and how they know that they cannot rely on their team coach to solve their problems and take their decisions. An action I took as a result of this was to have a badge that says *team member,* so I was wearing that during training sessions when I considered that what they were asking me to do was closer to what a team member does (for example to give them my straightforward opinion on how I believed something should be done, participate in energy raising games, etc.) than to my role as a team coach. That strategy gave me permission to be a team member but also showed them the difference in that role.

I found interesting results when I asked the team to describe our interaction with a picture or a word. As the literature indicates, their answers talked a lot about *the personality of the coach* (i.e. positive, friendly, honest, considerate, assertive, confident, inspiring). From other conversations I had with colleagues, this might be something cultural too, but I am also aware that I struggle not to show my emotions and feelings with them sometimes (verbally and non-verbally) but as Partanen (2012) indicates I used my personality as a tool to have crucial honest conversations. I also asked them to describe

*Table 2.2* My role as a CoP manager

| The Role of a CoP Manager | Examples Given by Students (The Coach Does This …) |
|---|---|
| Building and negotiating meaning | That happened recently when talking about respect. We had a conversation about what respect means to each of us (I1). <br> Yes, because if you are not on the same page, the team has different ideas of what they expect from the team and that could be quite dominating (I2) <br> Without doing too much telling us what this is, the team coach influences this (I3). <br> We are very individual so we have different meanings (I4) |
| Learning by doing | The coach always tries to find out the most about people and what interests them to learn during the process (I1) <br> From observations and giving us feedback (I3). |
| Articulating vision, goals, objectives, and activities | By making sure we are following our mission, vision and values and rules (I1) <br> Ensuring that we were setting ground rules, and making sure that we defined the mission, vision, and values to what Scion wanted to be as a team (I3) |
| Building trust and enabling collaboration | The coach always looks for us to work with new people and make sure that we are collaborating with each other such as through team projects (I1) <br> This is very important as you want a coach you can trust, be open with if you are having problems within the team. Collaboration from many things, with emails, looking over at project reviews, etc. (I2). <br> Making sure that we collaborate with other teams and we make the most of our training sessions and we are open and honest with each other (I3) <br> She definitely pushes us towards team projects. We might not move as fast as we could but it is definitely there" (I4) <br> My team coach is someone I can trust |

(*Continued*)

*Table 2.2* (Continued)

| The Role of a CoP Manager | Examples Given by Students (The Coach Does This …) |
|---|---|
| | and go for advice (documentary analysis). |
| Identification of individual CoP members' skills, talents, and knowledge | She gets to know everyone within the team and this comes to feedback as well. If you know them you can give better feedback (I2). |
| Creating synergies within the CoP | She is just another member of the team for this. If the people have the information this happens naturally (I4) |
| Developing relational resources | Pushing external communication quite well. She brings conversations that may be delicate but it grows your relation (I4). |
| Focus on intrinsic motivation | She is quite inspiring for intrinsic motivation. We all drop off that quite quickly but you will come and ask "what is the next step?" and push us towards progression (I4) |
| Setting challenges for individuals | The coach tries to push as or give us guidance on what we could do as a challenge or as a task (I1) |
| | If the coach sets the challenge and the team let's the coach down this usually has a bigger impact on the team. It is different when it does from the coach (I2) |
| | She is someone I can discuss problems with (documentary analysis). |
| Balancing constraints and freedoms and managing boundaries | The coach allows us a lot of freedom but at the same time she reminds people if they are not managing their time, or not doing … not what they should, but what they could be doing, opportunities that are there (I1). |
| | She does this and is important (I2) |
| | In training session if we go off a tangent or there is important stuff that we need to discuss there is guidance to speak about the topic (I3) |
| | She has a role on which are the constraints and freedoms. There will be times when people get away with something and you bring this up. She is very good giving |

*(Continued)*

*Table 2.2* (Continued)

| The Role of a CoP Manager | Examples Given by Students (The Coach Does This ...) |
| --- | --- |
| | freedoms, for example, we have weekly actions but then we are free to decide how we do that (I4) |
| Managing the power dynamics | Definitely yes (I2) |
| | This is team members' role too. The coach also tries the quiet ones to talk more, encouraging them to participate (I4) |
| | Our team coach is "a voice of reason" and a "critical view point" (documentary analysis).You always make sure all members are ok and that nobody is left behind (documentary analysis). |
| Setting the rules | No. The coach does not set the rules. We as a team set the rules but the coach sometimes will remind us of the rules we have set to see if we are following or not and if we are on track (I1) |
| | She helps us to ensure we were setting our ground rules, which we put in place to ensure that the team is focused and involved, open and honest, and building up safe and secure training session, responding each other with respect and manners (I3) |
| | This is something we have to do (I4) |
| Managing conflicts | The coach managed the conflict that we had with a project by speaking to all of us and making sure that we were aware of other people's feelings, in a set setting, within a training session. Then also reminding us about the positives and negatives that came from that (I1). |
| | They are not a teacher they are not telling people off but they make sure that it does not get out of hand. Or saying, "let's have 5 min and come back to this later", and re-energizing the team after a conflict (I2). |
| | People not volunteering to go to Wednesday's sessions. Trying the people to go there. Managing people |

*(Continued)*

*Table 2.2* (Continued)

| The Role of a CoP Manager | Examples Given by Students (The Coach Does This …) |
| --- | --- |
| | that are not attending or have conflicts in project teams (I3). |
| | The team members come to the resolution of the conflict, but I see the coach as 1 of the team members on this (I4) |
| Coach and role model | This as well. Someone to look up to that inspires the team. It is quite motivational (I2). |
| Face-to-face meetings and personal relationships | This is done by the coach trough 1 to 1s, leadership meetings, and by being around (I1). |
| | With the 1 to 1s which were very useful, and with personal relationships by being able to contact her, being accessible (I3) |
| | Really good I remember the summer's 1 to 1 was very very good (I4). |
| | My go-to person in times of need. Helped me stay on track and maintain a positive attitude, given me constructive criticism (documentary analysis). |

Source: Author's own.

my role and to indicate the things they would like me to do more or to do less. The feedback made me think about the level and content of my interactions, as, although concise and limited, could be seen as too directive and assertive at times. One of the transitions that I might have influenced (too much) is the shift from not having a leadership team to having one:

> *"You have a big impact on the structure of this team and how we organize"* (documentary analysis).

There were contradicting statements around my role, which reflects the different needs of the members and the expectations they have on the team coach. Some people thought I was being directive guiding them and providing information, others that I was facilitating just by prompting questions, and my role was more about providing support, feedback, and guidance. The reality is that both are fine, as we need to consider team coaching in context (TE) as there are frameworks and boundaries of what is expected of them from the programme. But, how do you meet the needs of the whole team when they have such different expectations? Contracting, i.e. developing a common understanding on what my role and their role within the team entails in terms of responsibilities, expectations, and working habits and behaviours, not only in the beginning of the engagement but throughout the coaching relationship. As Bennett (2008, p. 9) indicates, if assumptions are not aired and reconciled trouble can ensue, so contracting plays a crucial part in defining roles, desired results, but also established structure and processes.

From their feedback it was also quite evident that I inspire and ignite change and action by pointing out the needs of the team. I have quite a strong critical voice. Although I might see this as a strength (I see their potential for more), I need to be careful to do this through inspiring and positive questions, and positive compelling invitations.

I realized how important *trust* is. The team coach is the person that helps the team to learn, unlearn and search for options and meanings, but those dialogue sessions are much deeper if there is a climate of trust and they feel in a safe space.

One point that came out from both the documentary analysis and the interviews is that of *managing conflicts.* Some members thought that I should not bring up *touchy* subjects and *incidents.* This was challenged by other members that saw conflict as a source of learning. As a result of that discussion they decided to include in the contract something around my role that says: *building the capacity to manage conflicts positively: mediation and feedback to ensure that conflict is recognized (and use it beneficially)* and *outline problems when they arise*, which shows that they have come to an agreement of openness to discuss delicate issues as a source of learning.

## Conclusions

Although CoPs themselves are not a new concept, their existence in modern organizations is becoming more relevant as we move towards a democratization of the workplace and team-based management and leadership practices.

What seems clear is that some members of the team could be initially learning from the CoP by being on the *periphery* (observing, sharing experiences, etc.) and this sometimes encourage them to move towards the *centre* of the community to become more engaged members of it.

This implies that not only their experiential learning (from projects, ventures, etc.) is important, but that their constant and meaningful interactions within the TC through their training sessions are a crucial part of their entrepreneurial learning. Besides, their interaction with the whole TE CoP (a community of nine teams of 15–20 members each) is central in their learning and build a sense of identity towards the programme.

My coaching motto is *develop independent thinkers but inter-dependent actors* as I want them to think on their own and develop tools and strategies to voice their thinking, but act as a team and be aware that their actions influence and impact others. One thing I learnt is that I might have high expectations of the team and I somehow expect every member to be in the *core group* or be an *active member* of the CoP and learning community. This comes from my coaching philosophy and the *self-reflective* and *critical thinking me* which externalizes in many aspects of my practice. As Peters and Carr (2013, p. 5) point out, *"an excellent team coach keeps the team's highest aspirations and desired outcomes in mind"*. I understand that although I could see more potential in them and I wanted to motivate those more peripheral members to be more engaged, it is quite natural for a team to have different participation levels and I do not need to push this too much.

In addition, this research emphasized how important is the *contracting* process between the team coach and the team members. One of my biggest learning came when, as a result of my reflections of this study, I engaged with the learners in a feedback and contracting process that took place in several sessions. This gave us the opportunity to discuss leadership, their responsibilities as team members, as a team, my role as a team coach. The process culminated with a document that we all signed where we clarified our roles and expectations, as well as our functioning mechanisms (ground rules for training sessions, meetings, etc.) which gave us a framework for mutual accountability and responsibility, which I think is essential for a team to perform efficiently.

I hope this reflection serves other team coaches to take on board some of these considerations for their future practice and research. We should remember that whatever role we adopt, *"our job is not to prepare students for something; our job is to help students prepare themselves for anything"* (Spencer & Juliani, 2017, p. xxxiii).

# References

Akinoglu, O., & Yasar, Z. (2007). The effects of note taking in science education through the mind mapping technique on students' attitudes, academic achievement and concept learning. *Journal of Baltic Science Education,* *6*(3), 34–43.

Allee, V. (2000). Knowledge networks and communities of practice. *OD Practitioner,* *32*(4), 4–13.

Bennett, J. L. (2008). Contracting for success. *The International Journal of Coaching in Organizations,* *6*(4), 7–14. https://researchportal.coachfederation.org/Document/Pdf/2955.pdf

Borzillo, S., Aznar, S., & Schmitt, A. (2011). A journey through communities of practice: How and why members move from the periphery to the core. *European Management Journal,* *29*(1), 25–42. doi:10.1016/j.emj.2010.08.004.

Boyce, L. A., Jeffrey Jackson, R., & Neal, L. J. (2010). Building successful leadership coaching relationships: Examining impact of matching criteria in a leadership coaching program. *Journal of Management Development,* *29*(10), 914–931. doi:10.21236/ada524818.

Boyer, E. (1990). *Scholarship reconsidered: Priorities of the professoriate.* San Francisco, CA: Jossey-Bass.

Brown, S. W., & Grant, A. M. (2010). From GROW to GROUP: Theoretical issues and a practical model for group coaching in organisations. *Coaching: An International Journal of Theory, Research and Practice,* *3*(1), 30–45. doi:10.1080/17521880903559697.

Chu, M. T., Khosla, R., & Nishida, T. (2012). Communities of practice model driven knowledge management in multinational knowledge based enterprises. *Journal of Intelligent Manufacturing,* *23*(5), 1707–1720. doi:10.1007/s10845-010-0472-6.

Clutterbuck, D. (2011). *Coaching the team at work.* London: Nicholas Brealey Publishing.

Coghlan, D., & Brannick, T. (2005). *Doing action research in your own organization,* 2nd Edition. London: Sage.

Davey, T. (2017) *Tiimiakatemia (Team Academy). Team learning through starting a business at Tiimiakatemia.* Finland: Jyväskylä University of Applied Sciences.

Eden, C., & Huxham, C. (1996). Action research for the study of organizations. In S. Clegg, C. Hardy, & W. Nord (Eds), *Handbook of organization studies* (pp. 526–542). Thousand Oaks, CA.

Ferguson, L. M., Yonge, O., & Myrick, F. (2004). Students' involvement in faculty research: Ethical and methodological issues. *International Journal of Qualitative Methods,* *3*(4), 56–68. doi:10.1177/160940690400300405.

Flyvbjerg, B. (2006). Five misunderstandings about case-study research. *Qualitative Inquiry,* *12*(2), 219–245. doi:10.4135/9781848608191.d33.

Garavan, T. N., Carbery, R., & Murphy, E. (2007). Managing intentionally created communities of practice for knowledge sourcing across organisational boundaries: Insights on the role of the CoP

manager. *The Learning Organization, 14*(1), 34–49. doi:10.1108/096964
70710718339.

Healey, M., Flint, A., & Harrington, K. (2016). Students as partners:
Reflections on a conceptual model. Teaching & learning inquiry. *The
ISSOTL Journal, 4*(2). doi:10.20343/10.20343/teachlearninqu.4.2.3.

Hubert, C., Newhouse, B., & Vestal, W. (2001). *Building and sustaining communities of practice*. Houston: American Productivity Centre.

Lockett, N., Quesada- Pallarès, C., Williams-Middleton K., et al. (2017) 'Lost
in space': The role of social networking in university-based entrepreneurial
learning. *Industry and Higher Education, 31*(2), 67–80. https://doi.org/10.11
77/0950422217693962

Moingeon, B., Quélin, B., Dalsace, F., & Lumineau, F. (2006). Inter-
organizational communities of practice: Specificities and stakes. *Les Cahier
de Recherche, 857*, 18.

Nonaka, I., & Takeuchi, H. (1995) *The knowledge creating company: How
Japanese companies create the dynamics of innovation*. Oxford: Oxford
University Press.

Partanen, J. (2012) *The team coach's best tools*. Jyväskylä, Finland: Partus.

Peters, J., & Carr, C. (2013). *High performance team coaching*. Altona, Manitoba,
Canada: Friesen Press.

Pittaway L., & Cope J. (2007) Simulating entrepreneurial learning: Integrating
experiential and collaborative approaches to learning. *Management
Learning, 38*(2), 211–233. doi:10.1177/1350507607075776.

Pittaway L., & Thorpe R. (2012) A framework for entrepreneurial learning: A
tribute to Jason Cope. *Entrepreneurship & Regional Development, 24*(9–10),
837–859. https://doi.org/10.1080/08985626.2012.694268.

Roberts, J. (2006). Limits to communities of practice. *Journal of management
studies, 43*(3), 623–639. doi:10.1111/j.1467-6486.2006.00604.x.

Saunders, M., Lewis, P., & Thornhill, A. (Eds). (2015) *Research methods for
business students*, 6th Edition. Harlow-England: Pearson Educational Limited.

Senge, P. (1990). *The fifth discipline: The art and science of the learning organization*. New York: Currency Doubleday.

Spencer, J., & Juliani, A. J. (2017). *Empower: What happens when students own
their learning*. London: IMPress.

Teece, D. J., Pisano, G., & Shuen, A. (1997). Dynamic capabilities and strategic management. *Strategic Management Journal, 18*(7), 509–533. 10.1002/
(sici)1097-0266(199708)18:7<509::aid-smj882>3.0.co;2-z

Wang C. L., & Chugh H. (2014) Entrepreneurial learning: Past research and
future challenges. *International Journal of Management Reviews, 16*(1),
24–61. doi:10.1111/ijmr.12007.

Wenger, E., McDermott, R. A., & Snyder, W. (2002). *Cultivating communities
of practice: A guide to managing knowledge*. Harvard, MA: Harvard
Business Press.

Woodhead, V. (2019). How does coaching help to support team working? *The Practitioner's Handbook of Team Coaching*, 469–474. doi:10.4324/9781351130554-35.

Yin, R. K. (2009). Case study research: Design and methods. Thousand Oaks, CA: Sage. *The Canadian Journal of Action Research*, *14*(1), 69–71. doi:1 0.3138/cjpe.30.1.108.

# 3   Is It All in the Mindset?
# Team Coaching, Psychological Capital, and the Collaborative Development of an Entrepreneurial Mindset

*Carol Jarvis, Hugo Gaggiotti, and Selen Kars*

## Introduction

The changing nature of work attaches greater significance to the development of entrepreneurial capacities, with growing interest in entrepreneurial mindset and psychological capital. Psychological capital (PsyCap) includes measures of self-efficacy, hope, optimism, and resilience (Luthans et al., 2007). The notion of *entrepreneurial mindset* is less clearly defined but generally builds on Dweck's (2012) *growth mindset* to encompass additional measures such as social networks, risk-taking, and creative problem-solving.

Baluku et al. (2016) suggest PsyCap is a better predictor of entrepreneurial success than the amount of start-up capital available. Despite this, a recent study of 1,500 students found 88% of students felt they would leave university emotionally unequipped for *the real world of work* and 57% felt universities were not doing enough to equip them with these skills (Fika, 2019). The Team Academy (TA) approach seeks to address this, committing to the development and wellbeing of the individual, team, community, and ecosystem at the heart of its philosophy.

This chapter reports on our research into the development of PsyCap and entrepreneurial mindset among team entrepreneurs (TEs) on a UK TA programme. Our research approach, designed in the spirit of TA, encouraging co-creation and active participation from TEs and their team coaches, explored the interaction between learning environment – including space, micro-culture, team coaching, and team learning – and the development of entrepreneurial mindset and PsyCap. We provide critical insights into a *scholarship of practice* (Ramsey, 2014) and the influence of the *micro-cultures* in which these programmes are embedded (Tosey et al., 2015).

DOI: 10.4324/9781003163121-3

## Conceptual Framework

The increasing complexity of the nature of work and employment patterns increased interest in concepts such as entrepreneurial mindset and PsyCap. Luthans et al. (2007, p. 3) define PsyCap as a positive psychological state of development characterized by:

1   self-efficacy which is defined as having the confidence to attempt challenging tasks;
2   optimism which leads to positive affect and a high expectancy of success;
3   hope which involves the determination to achieve one's goals, including the flexibility to adapt one's approach to increase chances of success;
4   resiliency which involves sustaining efforts to achieve success in the face of obstacles and adversity.

As PsyCap is argued to be more *state like*, rather than *trait like* (Luthans & Youssef, 2007), it is deemed to be open to development.

The notion of *entrepreneurial mindset* is less clearly defined but generally builds on Dweck's (2012) *growth mindset* to encompass additional measures such as social networks, risk-taking, and creative problem-solving (Davies et al., 2015; Sidhu et al., 2016). Despite widespread usage of the term in practice, scholarly work is sparse, with limited criticality.

As a pedagogy in entrepreneurship education, critical practice, by experiential learning (Kolb, 1984), requires the entrepreneur to engage in a reflective critique of their experiences and assumptions by synthetically integrating multiple perspectives (Brechin, 2000). Brechin (2000) describes two guiding principles in critical practice relevant to entrepreneurship education: respecting others as equals, with interpersonal relationships as the starting point; and taking an open approach to working in uncertain environments. A reflexive cycle is created where critical action and critical thinking intertwine in critical practice. Understandings and actions are changed by actors' experiences with others, as they too influence and change others'.

Tosey et al. (2015) explore how this manifests in a Finnish university programme where the Tiimiakatemia/TA model was pioneered. They emphasize the importance of considering the "micro-culture" when seeking to adopt a pedagogy given its complex, emergent nature which makes it unamenable to efforts to influence, adapt, and transfer it. They identify four attributes contributing to the learning environment:

social embeddedness, real-worldness, identity formation, and norma-tive. Their Finnish case study notes the dominance of team/collective learning (social embeddedness), the increased level of *risk,* and the role of coaching and team learning in providing *psychological safety* (real-worldness). Membership of this community is symbolized through a distinctive language and dialogue among team members with an or-ientation towards entrepreneurial behaviour (identity formation) which is also sustained by the ideological practices communicated, diffused, and enacted through teaching and learning methods (normative).

When combined with TA's commitment to development and well-being, critical practice can approach *praxis* (Freire, 1972), where one engages as a committed thinker and actor with the intention to act truly. Ramsey (2014) develops this, arguing for a scholarship of practice that emphasizes paying attention to relations between ideas and action; inquiry which implies the idea of scepticism towards ac-tions and their implications; and the quality of relationships.

In this chapter, we explore how a scholarship of practice is enacted in a TA programme and its influence on the development of PsyCap and entrepreneurial mindset.

## The Research Site

Our research took place with TEs and team coaches on the BA Sports Business and Entrepreneurship programme, a 3-year undergraduate degree developed in partnership between the University of the West of England, Bristol and the Bristol City Robins Foundation (BCRF), a community-based educational trust established by Bristol City Football Club. It runs from a dedicated space in Bristol City's Ashton Gate Stadium, located in an area of low participation in higher edu-cation. The first cohort of TEs joined the programme in September 2017. Our research took place in the first year that the programme had all three year groups (October 2019–November 2020). There were 34 TEs on the programme, in which 25 participated in our research.

As with other chapters in this book series, the programme adopts the TA approach to learning entrepreneurship through doing (com-pleting, reflecting on, and evidencing learning from live projects). The educational philosophy, pedagogy, and techniques are described in detail elsewhere in this book and in Partanen (2012). TEs at BCRF are coached in team companies of up to 15 TEs, with each team enjoying two, 3-hour training sessions per week.

BCRF site has a number of distinguishing features considering Tosey et al.'s (2015) regard for micro-cultures. BCRF has a strong community focus (social embeddedness) and this imbues the programme and its culture. The stadium is a working environment (real-worldness), home to local sports clubs which adds another dimension to exposure to risk and the development of external networks and ways of working. The TEs at BCRF are adopting many of the ideological practices, team learning, dialogue, participation in learning journeys, and entrepreneurial behaviours (identity formation). Wellbeing of the individual, team, community, and ecosystem is at the heart of the programme's philosophy, as is an emphasis on critical self-reflection (normative).

## In Search of a Congruent Method

Our research adopted a mixed methods approach. Qualitative elements of the research aimed for congruence with the programme's underpinning philosophy; they were largely collaborative, team-based and, where TEs were involved, were treated as learning opportunities for the TEs, as well as the research team. Two co-creation workshops with 25 TEs and external entrepreneurs/entrepreneur advisors explored how TEs make sense of and interpret notions of entrepreneurship, team entrepreneurship, and entrepreneurial mindset. The third co-creation workshop (cancelled due to the pandemic) was replaced by a video competition inviting TEs to "pitch" their entrepreneurial attributes to a potential investor and a 360° feedback session based on entrepreneurial attributes identified in the co-creation workshops, providing depth of insight into how these attributes were interpreted and acted on. A PsyCap questionnaire administered one year apart was designed to provide insight into any shift in attributes as the TEs progressed through the programme and allowed for comparison with a control group of students. Three focussed discussion meetings with the programme staff provided a different perspective on the emerging themes and insights into staff skills and experience required to facilitate enquiry-led learning. This chapter pays particular attention to the learning from our research with the TEs, where visual methods were used for data elicitation.

Writers on visual methods are concerned with methods of generating and interpreting life visual experiences (Warren, 2002) and using the visual as an evidence of the social (Knowles & Sweetman, 2004). In our work, we considered the visual inseparable from everything experienced by participants at BCRF and, for us researchers, a means to accessing how TEs imagined and enacted entrepreneurship, in the process, described by Boje and Baskin (2011, p. 415) as creating meaning and picking out aspects of a complex, constantly changing reality which is a symbolic-interpretative process shaped by relationships, apparatus, practices, and discourses embedded in those relationships.

## *Visual Experiences*

To capture the social, processual, and dynamic nature of learning and creating meaning (Boje & Baskin, 2011), we embodied a methodology that prioritized visual experiences: LEGO® Serious Play™ model building, story-writing, asset mapping, storytelling, and video-making. Collecting data from the movement of hands as well as of mouths, attending the overlapping conversations and the spontaneous humour-jokes made when interacting alerted us to the richness of TEs' reflections. Faces, gestures, the use of hands accompanying the conversations unearthed contrasting perspectives and enabled rich reflection and reflexivity for us as well as the participants (Figure 3.1) (Gaggiotti & Gaggiotti, 2021).

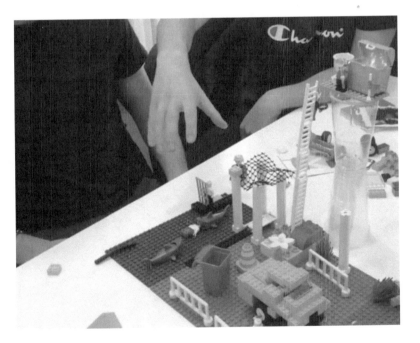

*Figure 3.1* Bodies and words.

Source: The Authors©.

Observing TEs producing artefacts in interaction with each other and us yielded insights impossible to capture through questionnaires and interviews. And the process provided insights into how a micro-culture learns. When analysing, this richer, more ambivalent, less word-dominated data better reflected the multidimensionality of an entrepreneurial mindset.

These visual experiences were produced in the TEs' own physical space: the stadium, the facilities, the meeting rooms. This redefined the traditional power relations between the researcher (i.e. lecturers) and the researched (i.e. "students"). TEs were comfortable in their own territory and we were alert to the space as well as what was happening in it. Here we discuss how we visualized (live, synchronous) and audio-visualized (based on recordings) two research events: a LEGO® Serious Play™ exercise (first co-creation workshop) and a mapping exercise (second co-creation workshop).

## Co-creation Workshops

The first co-creation workshop (November 2019) opened with a LEGO® Serious Play™ exercise where TEs worked in small teams to build models that represent entrepreneurial values. The images below illustrate the LEGO® models produced, most of which conceptualized the "entrepreneur as lone hero", and how students worked with and interpreted the task (Figure 3.2).

*Figure 3.2* Objects "showing" the nature of an entrepreneur. *This represents the top, the money. This is a person trying to climb the ladder.* [laughs].
Source: The Authors©.

*Figure 3.3* Paying attention to the details.
Source: The Authors©.

The movement of participants' fingers signposting and explaining the location and selection of objects was consistent with the ongoing nature of the entrepreneurial process of evaluating and re-evaluating ideas (Figure 3.3).

At some point the model collapsed; this was used as the perfect occasion to explain fragility and instability of entrepreneurial endeavours. The noise of the pieces collapsing, the exclamation, and surprise from participants help to reflect on the unexpected that could transform the entrepreneurial assumptions. "*We tried to support it, but we couldn't …*" (Figure 3.4).

Interestingly, TEs used objects sourced from the environment that were not LEGO® pieces to enhance their models: plastic glasses grabbed from the water dispenser to build a pedestal for the entrepreneur, other objects (e.g. a bigger, shinier trophy) and postcards borrowed from a previous activity to add a background image (e.g. a road) or enhance

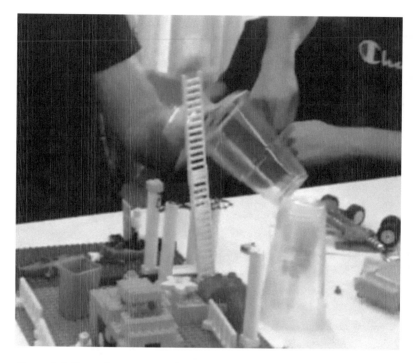

*Figure 3.4* Capturing unexpected experiences of entrepreneurship.
Source: The Authors©.

their message with motivational phrases (e.g. you make me believe in magic). The parallel with resource bootstrapping was noticeable and arguably evidenced an entrepreneurial mindset in-action even when attempting a non-contentious task like "take this suitcase of LEGO® pieces and build a model of ...".

## Reflecting on the Research Experience

In reflecting on and analysing the LEGO® models, as one of the co-researchers wrote in her field notes:

> *The theme was obvious, repeated itself again and again and we did not even need to hear the debriefing to reach a saturation point for data collection – the sole successful entrepreneur (literally) climbing the ladder of success (often with a sword or a treasure chest) after having*

*survived many dangers in the outside word ranging from sharks, to lions, to other entrepreneurs trying to catch him (always him!) out … there was only one way to succeed but many ways to fail.*

By contrast in the focussed discussions later in the day, where the TEs were exploring their own entrepreneurial experiences, learning, and development of their entrepreneurial attributes, she noted:

*Even though they mentioned that self-accountability and being responsible for their own learning were quite important they also recognised that they could not have learned everything by themselves and other teammates were key in their learning or in their inspiration and drive for learning.*

Or as one TE put it:

*even all sort of single heroes and that, they have people they work with or work with, in terms of their network … And then they've got employees. So, now that and their different personalities sort of require different needs.*

What emerged from these discussions was less about reaching the top, and more about adapting to new ways of learning and working; embracing the tensions between competing and collaborating, enquiry and advocacy, action and reflection, individual and team.

Through engaging with and embracing these tensions, without seeking a resolution, the TEs began to develop their entrepreneurial mindsets and PsyCap. Although numbers were small (only 11 TEs repeated it), findings from the PsyCap questionnaire showed development on all four measures of self-efficacy, hope, resilience, and optimism. The small sample size impacted on the ability to establish statistical significance. However, Effect Size Estimates (Cohen's D) indicated that the largest effect was for optimism, but all demonstrated a medium effect size and larger indications of change than those of the control group, with the exception of self-efficacy. We also note that the first data collection point (October 2019) was in a pre-COVID environment, whereas the second (November/December 2020) was during the COVID pandemic. It is likely that the pandemic impacts on levels of hope, optimism, resilience, and efficacy, as these all in some part are related with individuals' perceptions about their abilities to control and cope.

The discussions surfaced some of the ways in which the programme and its learning environment supported this:

> "*So, I think being an entrepreneur, surrounding yourself by other entrepreneurs and people with, that have high aspirations, is very important. But if I was on a different course with other people with a different mindset, I think I would struggle, because I think it would alter my mindset in a way … To not be as aspirational*".

> "*But the main things that I've sort of developed is confidence. Basically, because I've never been part of a real team, a consistent team previously, being part of a team where you're meeting two or three times a week and you've got sort of expectations for the team, I've just developed sort of the way I communicate with people. Developed sort of understanding of different personalities and characteristics*".

This also extended to the inter-relationship between project and academic work, which was seen to accelerate learning and enhance transferability of learning:

> *I think it's a good course to come to, because I didn't have the resources, knowledge and stuff to actually go out there and do it, this has given you platform to show me structure of how to do things. And actually, the assignments we had are targeted for giving us that knowledge, to actually understand it. So, they're not just pointless assignments, like these assignments teach you mindset and teach you entrepreneurial activities. Without the assignments, I don't think I'd have the knowledge I would today ….*

The mapping exercise undertaken in the second co-creation workshop (February 2020) deepened these insights with an opportunity to connect the development of an entrepreneurial mindset with programme elements. We generated 48 attributes associated with an entrepreneurial mindset, most mentioned by the TEs in the first co-creation workshop and the focussed discussion groups with some added from established external measures. Each TE had three dots to assign to the attributes they saw most important. The 12 that attracted the most "votes" were as follows: Drive, Risk-Taking, Motivation, Willingness to learn from failure, Adaptability, Resilience, Passion, Grit/persistence, Positivity, Creativity, Confidence, and Networker. These formed the basis for the mapping exercise, as captured in Figure 3.5.

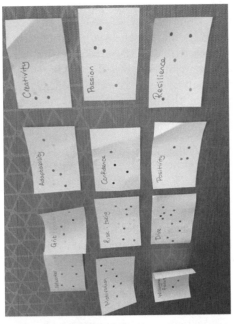

*Figure 3.5* (Compound of two pictures): The mapping exercise.
Source: The Authors©.

The "mapping exercise" surfaced new insights by getting TEs engage with the "messiness" of their learning experience, to make new connections between their learning, the entrepreneurial attributes, and their learning environment. Three attributes, resourcefulness, a desire to "fix" something, and "mental wealth" (labelled as looking after oneself and performing emotional first-aid as/when needed), were added and placed in the centre of the map, with a consensus that without mental wealth, none of the other attributes could flourish:

> *If you're not in a good space mentally, it's really hard to do any of these things, which can stop you progressing in any sort of form. Keeping yourself mentally there, like, keeping your wellbeing good, can lead to all these things.*

Thus, while none of the four dimensions of PsyCap (Luthans et al., 2007) were selected by the TEs in their 12 entrepreneurial attributes, it was implicitly seen as central to developing an entrepreneurial mindset.

With these observations, the dialogue became more generative (Isaacs, 1999) moving the emphasis from the individual and the structural aspects of the programme, to the collective and the relational; the relationships with fellow team members, team coaches, and social and professional networks in the programme and their role in developing entrepreneurial attributes. Figure 3.6 shows the connections uncovered.

The TEs also self-assessed their development against these 12 entrepreneurial attributes, comparing their scores when they started the programme with their scores now. They perceived having shifted most in their Willingness to learn from failure, closely followed by Networker, Risk-taking, and Confidence.

In keeping with our aim of conducting research in the spirit of TA the final year, TEs designed the attributes into a 360° feedback session (December 2020). Along with two team coaches, they scored each other against the attributes when they started on the programme and where they are now. Separately, the TEs were scored on a number of dimensions of engagement and performance by a team coach. Perhaps unsurprisingly, there was a relationship between the level of engagement and the development of entrepreneurial attributes. As team coaches observed in the staff discussion groups, coming to terms with the TA methodology can be challenging; it's an uncomfortable and unfamiliar approach to learning that requires commitment and participation to reap the rewards:

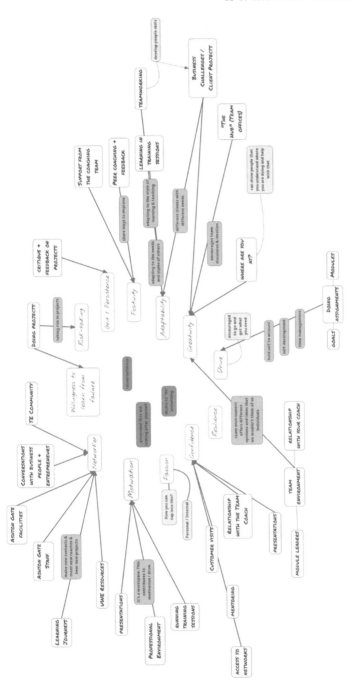

*Figure 3.6* Connections and their inter-relationships (the mapping exercise).
Source: The Authors©.

> 'why is there no lesson and why are they not teaching us anything?'
> and then once, you say, the penny-drop moment kicks in and they sort
> of realise, actually, we're responsible for creating our own course of
> action, and sometimes they come in and often there isn't a plan or, you
> know, a structure in place but they develop the skills maturity to then
> come in and actually think 'well, what are we doing today, what are
> we going to achieve, can ... you know, how can this benefit our long-
> term plan, our exit strategies?' And that then feeds into almost sort of
> an entrepreneurial mindset I guess in a way because as an entrepre-
> neur you're not ... you know there isn't somebody telling you what
> you're doing or telling you what you've got to do.

The numbers are too small to draw robust conclusions. However, as
highlighted in Figures 3.7 and 3.8, those who had the highest level of
engagement tended to score higher on their entrepreneurial attributes.
Also, their self-assessment was closer to the assessment of their peers
and coaches, whilst those who were less engaged tended to score
themselves higher than their peers and coaches did. Whether as an

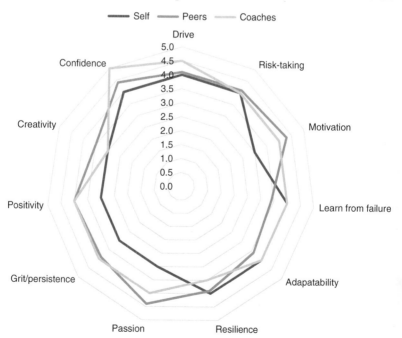

*Figure 3.7* Example 360° from highly engaged TE.
Source: The Authors©.

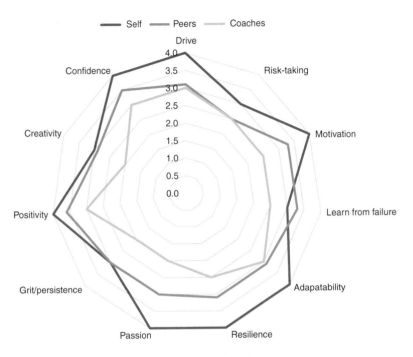

*Figure 3.8* Example 360° from less engaged TE.
Source: The Authors©.

entrepreneur or in the workplace, the capacity to reflect critically and accurately on your strengths and areas for development is a valuable and valued skill.

## Concluding Thoughts: It Is All in the Mindset but the Mindset Is Not All

The project demonstrated the importance of adopting congruent re-search methods that chime with the TA philosophy and approach which generated deeper engagement and learning for researchers and TEs, and favoured a programme micro-culture (Tosey et al., 2015). As one of the co-researchers noted, "*it was so striking that during the activities not a single student ever got their phone out or disengaged from the task for even a moment*".

Indeed, our method was not divorced from the field; it emerged from our interaction with the field. The method was used as an appreciative space, not just as a set of techniques for data collection and analysis. In this way, the research process became a research output itself. This approach helped different narratives to emerge, as with the contrasting narratives of the LEGO® exercise and focussed discussion groups. Multiple and non-singular narratives favoured the reflection of the differences between individual and group/team programmes. We realized that working individually we were not only drawn to the conception of the heroic, lone entrepreneur but we tended to focus on the uses of words as instruments with limited scope and bemoaning the relative absence of teaching. In contrast, the experience of building together, talking about an artefact (a model or a map) with others, helped to focus on the processual nature of the programme and the benefit of its unstructuredness. They paid attention to the team process and dynamics, to the texture of the "space", to the process and methodology. Their reflections were typically deeper and more creative. This was reflected in the language TEs used; it became more inclusive with the focus shifting to the relational and community.

As well as the tensions between individual and team/group/collective we observed the TEs embracing and navigating four types of tensions: enquiry and advocacy (fostered in particular through dialogue/training sessions); competing and collaborating; action and reflection; and the "academic" and the "practical". Methodology, relationships, and environment acted as a safety net that enhances learning (Tosey et al., 2015) through encouraging experimentation and embracing, rather than seeking to resolve tensions and fertile ground for the development of PsyCap.

## Further Research

In respect to the PsyCap, while the numbers are small to draw robust conclusions, we note that despite the impact of a pandemic, which has left its mark on mental, as well as physical, health, the TEs showed development on all four dimensions – self-efficacy, hope, optimism, and resilience (Luthans et al., 2007). There is scope for future research with a larger sample to explore this further.

Perhaps unsurprisingly, the 360° exercise suggested engagement as a reliable indicator of the development of entrepreneurial attributes, and also of the level of self-awareness. It would also be fruitful to explore this further.

The concepts of entrepreneurial mindset and psychological capital focus on the researcher on the cognitive. We suggest that in adopting a research approach that chimes with the spirit of TA, embracing the physical and embodied with the cognitive, we further the development of a scholarship of practice. Here is where we claim that it could be all in the mindset, but not only in the mindset. Through the TA approach, a lot is in the embodiment, the places, the micro-culture where experiences are contextualized.

## References

Baluku, M. M., Kikooma, J. F., & Kibanja, G. M. (2016). Psychological capital and the startup capital: Entrepreneurial success relationship. *Journal of Small Business & Entrepreneurship, 28*(1), 27–54.

Boje, D., & Baskin, K. (2011). Our organizations were never disenchanted: Enchantment by design narratives vs enchantment by emergence. *Journal of Organizational Change Management, 24*(4), 411–426.

Brechin, A. (2000). Introducing critical practice. In A. Brechin, H. Brown, & M. A. Eby (Eds), *Critical practice in health and social care* (pp. 25–47). London: Sage.

Davies, M., Hall, J., & Mayer, P. (2015). *Measuring the entrepreneurial mindset: Developing the entrepreneurial mindset profile (EMP)* [White paper]. Leadership Development Institute. https://www.emindsetprofile.com/wp-content/uploads/2015/10/EMP-White-Paper-Measuring-the-Entrepreneurial-Mindset.pdf

Dweck, C. S. (2012). *Mindset: Changing the way you think to fulfil your potential.* London: Robinson.

Fika (2019). Solve #MentalHealth crisis through emotional education. *FE News.* https://www.fenews.co.uk/press-releases/36159-solve-mentalhealth-crisis-through-emotional-education

Freire, P. (1972). *Pedagogy of the oppressed.* London: Penguin.

Gaggiotti, M., & Gaggiotti, H. (2021). Work, voice and reflexivity in audio-visual ethnography: Thinking through practice. In J. Pandeli, H. Gaggiotti, & N. Sutherland (Eds), *Organizational ethnography: An experiential and practical guide* (forthcoming). London: Routledge.

Isaacs, W. N. (1999). *Dialogue and the art of thinking together.* NYC: Doubleday.

Knowles, C., & Sweetman, P. (2004). *Picturing the social landscape: Visual methods and the sociological imagination.* London: Routledge.

Kolb, D. (1984). *Experiential learning as the science of learning and development.* Hoboken, NJ: NPH.

Luthans, F., & Youssef, C. M. (2007). Emerging positive organizational behavior. *Journal of Management, 33*, 321–349.

Luthans, F., Youssef, C. M., & Avolio, B. J. (2007). *Psychological capital: Developing the human competitive edge.* Oxford: Oxford University Press.

Partanen, J. (2012). *The team coach's best tools.* Jyväskylä: Partus.

Ramsey, C. (2014). Management learning: A scholarship of practice centred on attention. *Management Learning, 45*(1), 6–20.

Sidhu, I., Goubet, J., & Xia, Y. (2016). Measurement of innovation mindset a method and tool within the Berkeley Innovation Index Framework. *International Conference on Engineering, Technology and Innovation/IEEE International Technology Management Conference (ICE/ITMC)* (pp. 1–10). Trondheim: Norway.

Tosey, P., Dhaliwal, S., & Hassinen, J. (2015). The Finnish Team Academy model: Implications for management education. *Management Learning,* 46(2), 175–194.

Warren, S. (2002). Show me how it feels to work here. *Ephemera,* 2(3), 224–245.

# 4 Friend Leadership as a Novel Leadership Style

*Heikki Toivanen*

## Introduction

The new Generation Y (born 1977–1997) is now flowing into leadership positions and becoming new entrepreneurs (Tapscott, 2009). There are myths, stereotypes, and prejudices about the new generation (Tienari & Piekkari, 2011, p. 21) that influence how this new breed of leader might be perceived. However, we cannot escape the fact that the whole leadership paradigm is changing. The aim of this chapter is to offer a new leadership model of the leadership paradigm, which is called *Friend Leadership*. The term Friend Leadership is originally derived from a coaching program led by the founder of Tiimiakatemia Johannes Partanen at Tiimiakatemia in Jyväskylä, Central Finland. The content of Friend Leadership is inspired by the book *The Leadership Challenge* (Kouzes & Posner, 1995) and the HIT MR philosophy, that is to say, we should challenge process, have an inspirational vision, make actions viable, model the way, and encourage the heart. The term *friend* was translated from Finnish term *kaveri,* which actually means *fellow.* The key element of Friend Leadership is that the leader knows his/her subordinates better than acquaintances but less than close friends.

The Friend Leadership principles were created at Tiimiakatemia (Team Academy) during the training by Johannes Partanen (the head coach, the education councillor) and NJL (from Young Manager to True Leader-programme) in 2008, and the principles are as follows:

1  Be sensitive to people's emotions and act accordingly. As a friend leader, you must remember your own humanity.
2  As a leader, always be attentive and available, a genuine listener.
3  Only actions count in Friend Leadership.
4  The basic task of Friend Leadership is the leading of a learning

DOI: 10.4324/9781003163121-4

organization, and the needed basic skill is the ability to inspire others towards a common goal.

5  You can't lead others if you can't lead yourself.

6  In Friend Leadership, it is vital to set up playing positions for all in the team company, and to concentrate on their individual strengths. Team building skills are the absolute prerequisite for successful team leadership.

7  Everything rises and falls on leadership, and leadership falls on lack of communication.

8  Friend Leadership is never an award – it must be earned every day.

9  The friend leader's task is to create community positive thinking in the team company, together with its coach.

10  Friend Leadership is always setting an example. What you give your attention to, others will also.

## Leadership Change and the New Generation

Before discussing the research project that was undertaken to consider the use of Friend Leadership, it is helpful to consider the changes to leadership practices that have evolved because of the new generation of young leaders emerging. The new Generation Y is changing leadership practices. The commitment of the digital generation is much lighter – they are open-minded, multispectral, and interested in everything. Generation Y could also be called translearners (Tapscott, 2009) – they are present in many media at the same time and they learn in a novel way. The main medium for Generation X (born 1965–1977; Tapscott, 2009) is television, whereas for Generation Y and for Generation Z (born 1981–1984/6 and 1997–2012; Tapscott, 2009), it is the internet and mobile media. The TEs establish team co-operatives to learn leadership, team building, and especially entrepreneurship. The ownership in co-operatives offers an interesting focus for study relating to leadership practice. The ownership enables commitment, but it demands a new type of leadership because the traditional model of command and control does not succeed among the equal owners of a co-operative. The leadership dynamic is changing.

The present Generation Y (born 1977–1997) is totally different from Generation X (born 1965–1976) or baby boomers (born 1946–1964) (Tapscott, 2009). The coming Generation Z (born 1998-) is even weirder, they are not even capable of reading a newspaper anymore! They would attempt to zoom in on a picture in a printed newspaper in the same way that they might 'finger zoom' on a phone or tablet. The life of Generations Y and Z is concentrated around digital technology. Baby boomers and Generation X are, in turn, focused on television and newspaper. Tapscott (2009), Tienari and Piekkari (2011), Viljanen (2011), and Piha et al. (2012) have analysed the features of the new digital generation (Generations Y and Z) and have uncovered some commonalities. The smartphone is nearly an organic part of the digital generation, and the wireless network is a basic necessity that comes before food. The digital generation has grown up with interactive experiences. Everything needs to happen immediately.

The digital generation also has a relentless attitude to change the leadership principles in the working life. Tapscott (2009) describes the open world which Generation Y brings along into the working life and proposes four principles: collaboration, transparency, sharing, and empowerment. The operating learning framework used by Tiimiakatemia and Proakatemia, based on Nonaka and Takeuchi's knowledge theory (1995) supports Tapscott's principles because the learner constructs his/her own knowledge based on dialogue, reading, and doing. Learning is formed at stages of socialization, externalization, combination, and internalization. These principles can be observed in the co-operative members studied in the project which is explained later.

## Researching Leadership and Dialogue

Between 2012 and 2013, a research project has studied the leadership and dialogue processes of specific Generation Y groups working in co-operatives. The project was part of Finnish Government organization, TEKES's Liideri- business, productivity, and Joy at Work-Project 2012–2018. The research project was also part of a leadership in liminality space research project jointly with the University of Jyväskylä, Åbo Akademy, University of Helsinki, and University of JAMK University Applied Sciences. Liminality means the transitional period or phase of a rite of passage, during which the participant lacks social status or rank, remains anonymous, shows obedience and humility, and follows prescribed forms of conduct. The research project involved studying the Friend Leadership in students' final year bachelor theses. These students were team entrepreneurs (TEs), which is the term used in Tiimiakatemia for students. The TEs were all Generation Y students working in seven different cooperatives created as part of their programmes of study in Tiimiakatemia, based in Jyväskylä, and Proakatemia, based in Tampere, both in Finland. Both Proakatemia and Tiimiakatemia are based on the learning organizations model generated by Senge (1990): personal mastery, mental models, shared vision, team learning, and system thinking. Individual learning and searching for meaning and mastery as a team form the base for learning.

A comparative study was conducted in co-operatives at Mondragon University (in Basque, Spain). The dialogue quality of the teams was periodically measured, and statements were categorized according to the following axes: positive-negative, open-closed questions/statements, and others/us. Losada and Heaphy (2004) created a model to analyse the quality of dialogue and the level of the team. A high-quality team reaches the following statements: 6:1 in positive-negative, 1:1 in open-closed questions/statements, and 1:1 in others/us. In addition to these analyses, the leadership behaviour of teams and leaders was analysed by means of interviews, workshops, visual thinking based on frameworks of coaching leadership, non-leadership, deep leadership, and psychological capital.

What follows is an explanation of the Friend Leadership model as explored in the research, an indication of how the model relates to learning organizations, and some concluding thoughts about how the model might be further utilized.

## Friend Leadership Stairs Form a Core Model

Leading as a core function of organization can be crystallized as responsibility to reach the organizational target. The responsibility can be carried by the leader, the employee, or shared between the leader and the employee. If the leader takes the main responsibility, the organization operates like a Tayloristic (Seeck, 2008) machine. If the employees carry the main responsibility for the task, the organization is at a liminal stage, an unstructured organization. If both the employees and the leader are sharing the responsibility, the organization is in flow. There might be situations when strict leader discipline is required, like in the army, fire forces, or other security institutions. Then the leader must have crucial knowledge of leading. The organization might be needed to set up the liminal stage in situations of change, such as founding a new organization or laying off personnel. The liminal stage should only be formed for a limited amount of time.

Friend Leadership is an inspiring leadership model (Toivanen & Kotamäki, 2013; Toivanen, 2013) where the use of working power is genuinely agreed on between the leader and the organization. The organization has a shared vision; the leader needs to be more than an acquaintance, but less than a close friend. There are some dimensions in this system: graphic visualizations, positive psychological capital, and dialogue. In addition to these dimensions, some tools, like a visual leadership handbook, are created to facilitate the use of these dimensions. The core of the system is the shared vision. With the help of Friend Leadership principles, the organization finds and understands how it should use Friend Leadership in order to reach the shared vision. When the organization is in flow, the Friend Leadership stairs model can be seen in the middle.

The elements of the Friend Leadership stairs are based on Musashi's (1634) strategy book, and are as follows:

- Ground – lead yourself
- Water – form a crystal-clear shared vision of the team
- Fire – inspire the team
- Wind – create new elements in the business
- Void – mindfulness and understanding the meaning of spirit

In the following paragraphs, the five elements of the Friend Leadership stairs are discussed in more detail (Figure 4.1).

Leading oneself is the solid basis for the Friend Leadership stairs. According to Dee Hock (1999), 55% of leading is self-leading. Dee Hock also states that 20% of leading is leading colleagues, 20% is leading superiors, and only 5% concentrates on leading employees. The leader and the employee understand their own psychological capital: self-efficacy/confidence, hope, optimism, and resilience (Leppänen & Rauhala, 2012; Luthans & Youssef, 2004). Based on our research, young people seem to have strong optimism. Hope and resilience appear to be at the same level compared to older generations. On the other hand, people in their twenties seem to have less self-efficacy than people in their thirties. One way that Tiimiakatemia and Proakatemia enable a change in self-efficacy is through the learning contract. The learning contract (Cunningham, 1999) guides the personal mastery of development. The five key questions of a learning contract are: Where have I been? Where am I now? Where do I want to go? How do I reach my goal? How do I know that I have reached the goal? In his study, Cunningham (1999) concluded that the learning contract speeded up leader development. The leaders became aware of their own learning, needs, and targets. Motivation increased, self-confidence improved, business and strategy understanding developed, and positive attitude to learning progressed among the leaders studied by Cunningham (1999).

The second step of the stairs is to form a crystal-clear shared vision of the team. As in flowing water, the power of the team is enormous

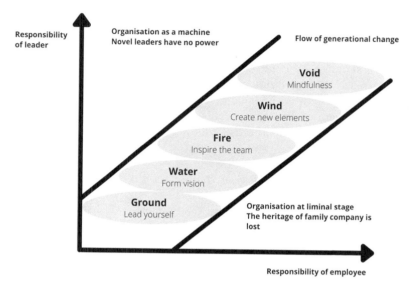

*Figure 4.1* Friend Leadership stairs.
Source: Author's own.

when the water drops are combined together. The team power is formed by positive dialogue. Dialogue (Greek *dia, logos*) refers to the meaning of the flow. It is a joint thinking session which forms the basis for further discussion and actions. There is no right or wrong side in good dialogue – just flow of joint thinking. Dialogue teaches us to see more than one single option and through this, the team members teach intelligence, power, and meaning to each other (Isaacs, 1999, p. 49, 64). Learning as a team is many times faster and more efficient than learning alone. The difference between the team members needs to be understood and utilized. Belbin et al. (1988) advise us to focus on the strengths of different kinds of team members. Belbin et al. (1988) defined nine different types of team roles, each of which plays a part in helping to create balance in a team. The team needs to have a vision in order to reach the target. Senge (1990) emphasizes the importance of the shared vision which he explains as being a way of creating a common sense of purpose and identity within a diverse community of people. The shared vision glues the team together.

The third step in the Friend Leadership stairs is to bring energy to the team. This is comparable to fire. A friend leader understands the key elements of deep leadership (Nissinen, 2001) which are building confidence; inspiring a way to motivate; learning and respecting. From another perspective, a friend leader knows Kouzes and Posner's (2007) leadership principles: (1) model the way; (2) inspire a shared vision; (3) challenge the process; (4) enable others to act; and (5) encourage the heart. Basically, a friend leader is a leader of sensibleness with heart. He/she is searching for a solution, not problems. A good friend leader is also acting without notes. He/she is like a leader of a jazz musician orchestra.

The fourth step in the Friend Leadership stairs is to create new elements in the business, this is understanding the power of wind. The hedgehog concept (Collins, 2001) guides the team to find the salient point in the middle of three circles: what is the team deeply passionate about; what can the team be best at in the world; what does one's economic engine drive one towards. The questions can be limited at one's own level of business operating area. Defining the strategy profile (Kim & Mauborgne, 2005), crystallizing the brand envelope and the unique sales promise (Gad, 2001), and visualizing the value chain (Osterwalder & Pigneur, 2010) provide the directions to business development.

The fifth step is the void which refers to mindfulness and understanding the meaning of spirit. This means profound perceiving of the strategy path as a part of the ecosystem and nature. When the power of nature is comprehended and the rhythm of all situations is felt, winning is natural. The symbols of nature need to be recognized – the visual measurement of business is a natural part of Friend Leadership. The crucial element in this step is mindfulness: be present where you are. This also means becoming aware of the spirit of the game where the team is playing. There are positive, negative, and neutral games. All the efforts should be realized to transform the spirit into something positive.

## How Friend Leadership Operates in Learning Organizations

Seeck's (2008) view of a definition of leadership includes consideration of the leader's role in supporting and focusing people's energies and interests into achieving a common goal. In the Friend Leadership model, the relationship is more equal where the vision owner leads with her/his own volition, and the power dynamic is genuinely agreed on between the leader and the organization. Friendship is the central theme in Friend Leadership. The leader needs to be more than an acquaintance, but less than a close friend.

As a leadership trend, Friend Leadership is close to coaching and shared leadership. The key element in coaching leadership is to coach the performance. The leader coaches others to clarify their targets and develop in their career (Kansanen, 2004). The core themes of shared leadership are to distribute tasks and to have joint actions. Shared leadership is sharing knowledge, experience, thoughts, appreciation, and confidence. Responsibility, polyphonic dialogue, and physical space guide everyone to take part in this kind of leadership (Ropo et al., 2005). Tienari and Piekkari (2011) highlight the inspiring term "non-leadership" as a way to lead Generation Z. Non-leadership is a contrast to more traditional leadership practices. Traditionally, leaders were seen as heroes and people would stand on ceremonies around them. The Generation Z leaders are kind of non-leaders, they conduct the leading task and then join the others in the team. In contrast, Tienari and Piekkari (2011) propose that leadership should be hidden. However, a friend leader is not hidden; he or she is a part of team, in a visual and inspiring way.

As a part of the *Leadership Challenge* book project, Kouzes and Posner (1995) conducted a study on the global leader's key features during the past three decades. The key features of the leaders are honesty, forethought, and an inspiring and competent ability. Based on the study, Generation Y has evaluated the features almost in the same way, except for the competent ability. The competent ability changed into a co-operative attitude based on the research. Instead of being competent, the leader for generation Y needs to cooperate. This can be seen in the way that the leader in a Tiimiakatemia or Proakatemia cooperative, and the organization define the performance equally; this is the difference between Friend Leadership and coaching or shared leadership.

The co-operatives are an excellent learning platform thanks to the limited initial capital requirement: it costs around 50 euros to register. From an owner's point of view, the co-operatives also offer the structure to have equal decision-making for all members. The dual role of the TEs as owners and employees creates an interesting stage for leadership observation. The co-operatives are formed on the basis of Belbin's team role tests (Belbin et al., 1988), gender, and special know-how. The co-operatives are akin to an ideal communitas. The term communitas refers to an unstructured and solitary community where the members are equal and free. There is a special communal and intense spirit in a communitas. In the Tiimiakatemia and Proakatemia programmes, selecting the management group or operating in smaller teams structures the co-operatives and leadership changes at least every year. The culture of Tiimiakatemia and Proakatemia offers a safe environment for leadership trials. For example, sometimes the team members or leaders are not operating according to the team norms and this might result in the team expelling a member or the leader which returns the team close to an original liminal stage, an unstructured form. If the leader or the management group keeps strict discipline, the team operates like a machine. Communitas (Turner, 1986, 2008, 2012) as a part of liminality is a very interesting approach through which to observe the organization and its leadership.

## How to Utilize Friend Leadership

Kuusisto and Kuusisto (2008) emphasize the importance of company culture which can transform when new leadership is in place. It is crucial to understand the stages of change and accept the change of company culture in order to ensure that the organization continues to function effectively and productively. The main target of the research project was to find out the functional leadership practices and styles for Generation Y and, most importantly, figure out how the older generation can benefit from paying attention to the key features of the new leaders.

Companies that act as learning organizations will be able to adapt to leadership change more easily and this is because a learning organization is committed to developing people's skills voluntarily at all levels (Senge, 1990). Traditional leaders in organizations need to understand the new generation and themselves as crucial parts of the company transformation process: as individuals, as leaders, and partners in thinking and dialogue. A shared vision for the leadership change project is required between the old and new leaders in order for them to achieve smooth transformation. The old leaders in particular need to understand the requirements of the new leaders because it is the latter that has the power to implement change.

There are three stages in the generation change of a leader:

1   Preparation stage
2   Shared leadership stage
3   Independent leadership stage (Kuusisto & Kuusisto, 2008)

At the preparation stage of the generation change, the old generation has the leading role. The company is the child of the old generation leaders. Emotions are mixed with hard strategy facts: the company is the end result of the leader's career. It is important for the old leader to decide that *I am now preparing to make a strategic move to transfer my company!* Different types of trials to find new leaders at the preparation stage with the new generation are allowed. The key issue in the generation change is the values of the company and the old owner. The old owner can proceed in the company and take the first step of Friend Leadership stairs and write his/her own learning contract.

At the shared leadership stage, a team of new owners is selected. At this stage, the former and the new owner can proceed to the second and third steps of the Friend Leadership stairs. The common values, vision, and mission are crucial. The true meaning and purpose of the company are very important for Generations Y and Z. The purpose of the company that was important to the old generation might be totally different for the new generation. The way to operate and to work has also changed. The new generation requires open dialogue and enough room to act. Therefore, the old generation needs to transfer the leadership genuinely to the new generation. The duration of the shared leadership stage should be rather short, and the responsibilities should be defined and communicated clearly.

At the independent leadership stage, the old leader needs to be just a coach and act only when the new generation is asking for advice. The new leaders can move to the fourth and fifth steps of the Friend Leadership stairs. Emotionally, this stage might be tough for the old leader, but the role as a spare advisor needs to be accepted. The common values, mission, and vision between the new and old leaders defined at the shared leadership stage have now an important role. Generations Y and Z will lead the company to a new glory that they deserve – towards a better world.

## Concluding Thoughts

The research indicated a number of behaviours associated with Friend Leadership that were evident in the cooperatives created in both Tiimiakatemia and Proakatemia. In both cases, the organizations created acted as learning organizations and operated with the following principles:

1   When performing tasks, responsibility and initiative comes in balance between the organization and its members.
2   The organization has a genuine shared vision.
3   The organization is a community, that is to say, it is a community with an "us" spirit and rituals.

4    The members of the organization are friends with each other, more than acquaintances, but less than a close friend in the traditional sense, suits perfectly.

The elements of the Friend Leadership steps are vital to the success of a learning team. Earth is the establishment of operation. The friend leader identifies their own and their team's resources, weaknesses, and strengths. Water is crystal clear. Water is as powerful as a Tsunami or as a tiny drop. With the aid of positive dialogue, the organization forms a shared. Fire, that is to say, Friend Leadership, ignites the team. The power of fire can be large or small. Wind comes from another land. Workplace environment observation creates the foundation of success. The most important element is void: Presence, an understanding of the essential. The thought of it, what is known and what is not. Friend Leadership is understanding the team.

## References

Belbin, M., Belbin, N., & Bainbridge, D. (1988). *Belbin team roles.* http://www.belbin.com. Viewed 12.1.2014.

Collins, J. (2001). *Good to great.* New York: HarperCollins Publishers.

Cunningham, I. (1999). *The wisdom of strategic learning: The self-managed learning solution* (2nd ed.). London: Routledge.

Dee Hock, B. (1999). *Birth of the chardiordic age.* San Francisco: Koehler Publisher.

Gad, T. (2001). *4-D branding.* London: Prentice Hall.

Isaacs, W. (1999). *Dialogi ja yhdessä ajattelemisentaito (Dialogue and joint thinking ability).* Jyväskylä: Gummerus kirjapaino.

Kansanen, P. J. (2004). The role of general education in teacher education. *Journal of Educational Science, 7*(2), 207–218. doi:10.1007/s11618-004-0022-0.

Kim, W. C., & Mauborgne, R. (2005). *Blue ocean strategy.* New York: Harvard Business School Publishing.

Kouzes J., & Posner, B. (1995). *The leadership challenge.* New York: Wiley & Sons.

Kuusisto, M., & Kuuisisto, T. (2008). *Johtaja vaihtuu –sukupolven kriittiset tekijät (Leader Changes – The critical factors of generation change).* Helsinki: Talentum.

Leppänen, M., & Rauhala, I. (2012). *Johda ihmistä. Psykologiaa johtajille (Lead the human being. Psychology for leaders).* Helsinki: Talentum.

Losada, M., & Heaphy, E. (2004). The role and positivity and connectivity in the performance of business teams. *The American Behavioral Scientist, 47*(6), 740–765.

Luthans F., & Youssef C. M. (2004). Human, social, and now positive psychological capital management: Investing in people for competitive advantage. *Organizational Dynamics, 33*(2), 143–160.

Musashi, M. (1997) [1634]. *Go rin no sho – Maa, vesi, tuli, tuuli ja tyhjyys (Ground, water, wire, wind, void)*. Keuruu: Otavan kirjapaino.

Nissinen V. (2001). *Sotilasjohtaminen. Kriittiseen konstruktivistiseen oppimiskäsitykseen perustuva johtajakoulutus Suomen puolustusvoimissa (Military leadership. Leadership training based on the critical constructive learning understanding in Finnish Defence Forces)*. Unpublished doctoral thesis. Helsinki, Finland: Helsinki University.

Nonaka, I., & Takeuchi, H. (1995). *The knowledge-creating company, how Japanese companies create the dynamics of innovation*. New York: Oxford University Press.

Osterwalder, A., & Pigneur, Y. (2010). *Business model generation*. New Jersey: John Wiley & Sons.

Partanen, J., NJL (Nuoresta johtajasta liideriksi 8 – ohjelma) (2008). *Kaverijohtamisen periaatteet. Tiimiakatemian osuuskuntien johtamistyökalut (Friend leadership principles, the leading tools of co-operatives in Tiimiakatemia)*. Jyväskylä: Tiimiakatemia (JAMK).

Piha, K., Puustell, A., Catani, J., Poussa, L., Varis, E., Tuhkanen, S., & Heinonen, M. (2012). *Dialogi. Uusi työ on täällä terveisin Y (Dialogue. New work is here, regards Y)*. Helsinki: Multiprint.

Ropo, A., Eriksson, M., Sauer, E., Lehtimäki, H., Keso, H., Pietiläinen, T., & Koivunen, N. (2005). *Jaetun johtajuuden särmät (Shared leadership corners)*. Helsinki: Talentum.

Seeck, H. (2008). *Johtamisopit suomessa taylorismista innovaatioteorioihin (Leadership paradigms from Taylorism to Innovation theory)*. Helsinki: Gaudeamus.

Senge, P. (1990). *The fifth discipline*. London: Century Business.

Tapscott, D. (2009). *Grown up digital*. New York: McGraw Hill.

Tienari, J., & Piekkari, R. (2011). *Z ja epäjohtaminen* . Helsinki: Talentum.

Toivanen, H. (2013). *Heippa, Pomo – onkos sulla muka mitään visioo? Y-sukupolvi päräyttää johtamisen kaverijohtamisen moodiin! (Hi Boss - do you supposed to have any vision? Generation Y will blow up the leadership at new mode!)*, TEKES in raportti 6/2013. Helsinki: Tekes.

Toivanen, H., & Kotamäki, M. (2013). *Kaverijohtamisen visuaalinen innostuskirja (Inspiriting visual friend leadership book)*. Jyväskylä: Jyväskylän Ammattikorkeakoulu/Pellervo.

Turner, E. (2008). Exploring the work of Victor Turner: Liminality and its later implications. *Suomen Antropologi: Journal of the Finnish Anthropological Society, 4*, 26–44.

Turner, E. (2012). *Communitas: The anthropology of collective joy*. New York: Palgrave Macmillan.

Turner, V. (1977). Variations of the theme of liminality. In S. Moore & B. G. Myerhoff (Eds), *Secular ritual* (pp. 36–51). Assen, The Netherlands: Van Gorcu.

Turner, V. (1986). *The anthropology of performance*. New York: PAJ Publications.

Viljanen, P. A. (2011). *NO FEAR Johtaja kohtaa digicowboyt (NO FEAR the leader faces Digital Cowboys)*. Helsinki: WSOYPro Oy.

# 5 Part I: The Phenomenon of "It" as Leadership in the Team Academy Model: Context and Overview

*Karolina Ozadowicz*

## Introduction

The Team Academy-based programmes offer a very particular context within which leadership emerges. The main building blocks of the Team Academy environment are self-managed entrepreneurial teams, consisting of members being on average 18–22 years old. Each of these teams is supported by the Team Coach whose role is to enable and facilitate the learning generated within each particular group. Although most programmes are based in the university setting, they are student-led. This means it is ultimately students who make decisions and take responsibility for their actions. The programme itself is practise orientated with each team member tasked to engage with real business challenges. Understanding this particular context within which leadership is studied is of key importance. Previous research demonstrated it is the context which shapes leadership and to understand the phenomenon of leadership accurately leadership must be studied with the respect and understanding of the environment within which it emerges (Porter & McLaughlin, 2006).

This short introduction to the concept of leadership in entrepreneurship teams, as explored in the context of the Team Academy-based programmes, is aimed at starting a dialogue on the subject so that further perspectives and observations can be shared, gathered, and discussed.

To achieve clarity of the discussion, first, an overview of the concepts of leadership in the general terms will be provided followed by the priority given to the context in which it occurs, i.e. entrepreneurial teams operating using Team Academy principles dialogue and circle processes.

The notion of leadership will be explored using examples and reflections gathered during the author's involvement with the programme, in

DOI: 10.4324/9781003163121-5

particular, the Team Academy-based programme placed in the University of the West of England, Bristol, called *Team Entrepreneurship*. This article is based on the analyses of the author's reflective journal entries since joining Team Entrepreneurship in 2015.

## Leadership in the Team Academy-Based Programmes

Although the majority will still perceive leadership from a singular perspective, Ciulla (1995) writes leadership is not a person or a position but rather a complex moral relationship between people, based on trust, obligation, commitment, emotion, and a shared vision of what is good.

In this chapter, I propose that the concept of leadership builds on an understanding similar to Ciulla's. Leadership is seen as a result of interaction between the individuals; it is a process which is complex, dynamic, and situational. Most distinctively, it is a process happening between people, resulting from the relationship between these individuals and of collective nature.

Perhaps the easier way to think of leadership is to use a pronoun where leadership is not *You* or *I*, but all of us, i.e. *We* in interaction with each other.

The conceptualization of leadership as something more than the action of one person goes back to the work of Stogdill and Shartle (1948) who argued that leadership is *"a process of interaction between persons who are participating in goal-oriented group activities"* (p. 287).The next major step towards theories of collective leadership was the work around the theories of followership (Baker, 2007) with leadership viewed as an effect of dyadic interactions and the notion of the giving and granting of leadership between team members. Based on such conceptualization, the assumption was that there is a reduced distinction between leader and follower, as each team member is able to fill either of these roles at any given time.

Relaxing the assumption that leadership is a property of individuals moved researchers into the direction of collective leadership where it is a team itself who carries out the leadership role. The focus of leadership studies moved from purely exploring leadership as a product to considering it as a dynamic, interactive and contextually embedded process of leading-following (DeRue et al., 2011).

Over the last two decades, the understanding of leadership as a collective process generated more and more interest contributing to the development of numerous theories of collective leadership. Some of the most well known include shared leadership (Pearce & Conger,

2002), team leadership (Zaccaro et al., 2001), distributed leadership (Spillane, 2005), complexity leadership (Uhl-Bien et al., 2007) or network leadership (Carter & Dechurch, 2012).

Shared leadership (sometimes referred to as network leadership) investigates leadership by analysing the strength and number of leadership connections as occurring within the collective. Team (also known as a group) leadership prioritizes analysing leadership with the focus given to the team processes itself. Distributed leadership (often confused with shared leadership) is a form of shared leadership where leadership action is generated and co-created by all team members contributing to the process with similar strength and frequency. Complexity leadership studies leadership as a result of multiple factors both external and internal, with leadership seen as a dynamic and ever-changing process of emergence.

Usually, more than one of these theories might interact with each other, and many can be used simultaneously as a means of describing leadership in teams (e.g. distributed leadership approaches mingle with formal styles of leading and complexity leadership). Although, as pointed by Yammarino et al. (2012), each of these theories has unique features, several similarities are cutting across all of them. This creates yet another challenge for studying leadership as it adds to the complexity of how leadership should be studied and understood. Further, perhaps it is safest to assume that each of the collective theories of leadership provides a good starting point for analysing leadership as occurring in the context of the Team Academy-based programmes.

Since the start of the Team Entrepreneurship programme in Bristol, there were noticeable difficulties with and ineffectiveness of collective leadership. Although the nature of the programme promoted leadership which was very *encompassing, equal,* and *fair* (as described by students in reflections), the collective leadership was also *slow, inefficient* and most importantly created this feeling of *inaction* where *officially everyone is responsible, but no one is.* It seemed the main *pain* of leadership related to students' inability to generate *collective responsibility.* This meant although discussions were rich and decisions had been made, there was no collective accountability and most of the time, no action or at best, the mediocre performance later on.

Around 2017 Team Coaches on Team Entrepreneurship programme in Bristol decided to encourage each team to appoint a formal leader so that at least one person per team would be responsible for the quality of team performance. As mentioned, all the teams on the programme are self-managed and ultimately it's the team members who make all of the decisions regarding their teams themself.

Regardless of the encouragement for teams to introduce formal leadership, several different choices have been made. Some teams decided to continue with distributed leadership (this choice seems to be especially popular with year 3 students, the most experienced and mature learners on the programme), whereas year 1 students most often chose to follow their coach's suggestion opting for more structured and formal leadership.

No clear-cut evaluation can be formed of the effectiveness of the choices made. However, it seems, these almost instinctive choices of *what leadership we are going for* were exactly what each team needed with the decisions made in alignment with the level of the development of each particular team. For example, year 3 students, having three years of experience of self-organizing, are most of the time able to generate enough *collective responsibility* with no need for a formal leader to tell them what they should be doing. Leadership in Year 3 teams is based on strong personal relationships with each student aware of each other's strengths and weaknesses. It is important to note, at times students even in Year 3 might opt to have a formal leader. However, most often it is not because they need one but rather that e.g. a particular person expressed a desire to practise the art of leadership and the team allowed them to do so (see more on this in Chapter 2).

Although the programme is advertised as *team focused*, a significant number of students still decide to develop so-called *individual projects*. They will work on their own without the team's support. Often these particular students will be so focused on developing their idea they will show little interest in anything else, perceiving it as a *danger* pulling them away from what matters to them most. This often leads to resistance to build the team (managing people takes time and students prefer to use this time to build their project instead), ultimately missing out on the opportunities to learn the processes of collective leadership (this might vary in other team academies and relate to the culture with the UK having more individualistic than e.g. Finland). The Team Academy-based programmes operate from the perspective that entrepreneurial initiatives sooner or later will require teams to support their ideas and hence the single entrepreneurs are rather discouraged by the programme.

The building block of all Team Academy-based programmes is that each entrepreneur needs to have at least a basic understanding of the skill of collective leadership. Often it is a role of the Team Coach to remind a student about the importance of creating a team and experimenting with leading it. Students are being made to realize, even if their *one-person* project will turn out successful, acquiring investors might be challenging as the majority of them will refuse to invest in the idea with no team (Holmberg-Wright & Hribar 2016). Further, selling such *one-person* companies is also difficult as such businesses are left with no one to run them except the founder who is the only person with expertise in how to do it.

The Team Academy programmes are students' led, and although the expectations of working with the team are communicated and asked for (e.g. through the team assignments with high weighting in terms of academic credits and encouragement for more team ventures and projects), each student's decision is respected even when that decision is contradictory to the expectation formed. In these particular instances when the student decides to continue with a *one-person* approach, such students are still encouraged to reflect on the concept of leadership but from the angle of *personal mastery* (García-Morales et al., 2006) and *self-leadership* (D'Intino et al., 2007). Often, such *single* entrepreneurs at some point are faced with the need of creating a team anyway (that is if their *one-person* idea works and they must create a team to develop their project further or because their project failed they must join another team to continue on the programme). Interestingly, such *single* entrepreneurs often become a key member of the collective leadership processes. Their leadership effectiveness is attributed to the time and effort they put into building and enhancing skills of *self-mastery* and *self-leadership* with both of these translating into the quality of their contributions to collective leadership processes later on. The calibre of individual contribution to the leadership process is of key importance. That is as the collective leadership is nothing more but the accumulated result of the quality of interactions between the individuals.

Although all Team Academy programmes are based on the same principles, there are noticeable differences between individual programmes. One of such differences relates to the construct of so-called team companies. As the context is known to impact leadership, any differences between basic components of the Team Academy programmes can offer clues about what supports and what hinders the process of creating effective leadership. It seems important to study these differences and the results they create.

Although there are differences in terms of how team companies are constructed, the team companies themselves do exist in most of the team academies. They remain the main instrument of learning enabling students to gain specific knowledge in two key areas: team (teamwork) and company (business) (hence *Team Company*). All students are allocated to a specific Team Company at the start of the programme and remain their members for the duration of their education. Each Team Company consists of up to 20 members. Usually, a Team Company will be given a financial target to meet during each academic year which will increase to correspond with the advancements of the students' skills. Achieving the financial target will be the Team Company primary focus, driving the actions of its team members throughout the programme.

The *Team Entrepreneurship* programme in Bristol decided to re-evaluate the purpose of the Team Companies. This was a thought-through decision aimed at increasing engagement, level of personal responsibility, as well as the intensity of knowledge creation. Financial targets had been removed and instead, students were encouraged to treat their Team Companies as *learning organizations* with the Team Company primary objective moved to facilitate students' learning. In practice, students would meet in their Training Sessions (teams' twice-weekly meetings) and one by one share information and learning from the various projects they are involved in outside of the Team Company. This shift in the main purpose of the Team Company (from business/income to sharing learning) brought implications for the leadership processes. The push to create collective income, product, or service disappeared and the role of the Team Company and Training Sessions turned into this obligation *to come in because there is this expectation I should.* As noted by one of the students regarding his resistance to engage with the Team Company:

> *The most difficult is not the leading itself but the first step of making that choice of wanting to lead. I don't feel like I want to. The rewards are little and responsibility is huge. It makes sense to me to simply not engage as my priorities are different. I mean I can lead on the project but I don't want to lead the team. No gains for me there.*
> (Student A, 2017)

This sharing was captured during 1-2-1 coaching sessions at the start of 2017. It felt important to be included as the reflections picturesquely describe challenges the change in the purpose of the Team Company construct brought, i.e. students struggled to appreciate the value of the Team Company and did not engage in the team processes by simply not coming in. In the academic year of 2020, the reflections on these challenges let the Team Entrepreneurship introduce new program design where financial targets were re-introduced.

One of the challenges faced by the coaches is low attendance in the training sessions leading to the goal of *shared learning* compromised to sharing between a few students only. Coaching in such a team is challenging as even if students come in, most often the style of their leadership is that of laissez-faire with the whole team unable to generate and sustain *collective responsibility*. The effect of this is that even the most motivated members can lose their willpower and there might be times where the whole team becomes leadership-less. These times are most dangerous for the cohesiveness of the group and often materialize themselves with the drop of attendance in the training sessions.

Next to leadership developing the Team Company, there is also another type of collective leadership often observed on the Team Academy programmes, i.e. project leadership. Project teams are the most common type of teams on the Team Academy-based programmes. These teams are initiated and created by the student, with the purpose to develop a particular product or service. Students join and leave these teams of their own accord based on their own interests and priorities. The purpose of the Project Teams is always this of creation/achievement with the financial goal always present (even if the project is a charity and the financial goal is to fundraise). There seems to be a natural allying between the team's purpose and the main *drives* energizing the teams' members (entrepreneurs are action and achievements orientated). For the leadership process, this alignment of the purposes creates implications, i.e. there seems to be no resistance to taking part in the leadership processes with everyone interested in taking responsibility for the success of the project. It's important to note that the lack of resistance to leadership processes does not mean there are no difficulties or challenges to leadership. They still exist but their character is different to those observed in the Team Companies (e.g. leadership in project teams might more often be exposed to power struggles or conflicts, whereas Team Companies suffer from lack of responsibility and resistance to participation).

In the Project Teams, in contrast to Team Companies, stakes are too high not to care (i.e. if successful all team members' goal of achievement and creation will be met). This in turn translates to everyone willing to contribute towards the effectiveness of their teams. The care is given to the Project Teams with the attitude of *I want to* and *I will* rather than *I must* or *I have to*. Leaders who co-create leadership processes from a place of care, genuine interest, and dedication have greater chances of experiencing richer learning. This is what we call *learning by doing* and what all Team Academy-based programmes aim towards. By *giving* and *contributing* students *learn on the job* acquiring the hardcore skills but also learning about themselves as leaders and the leadership as occurring in their teams. This in time makes these students even more effective ultimately leading to a greater chance of creating successful projects in the future.

So far, several observations had been made regarding phenomena of leadership understood as a collective process and as occurring in the Team Academy-based programmes. However, one important area so far not discussed relates to the so-called *black box* of leadership (Conger, 2004), i.e. what leadership actually is? What are the exact forms of leadership? Is it exercising influence? Is it making decisions? Motivating (empowering) people to achieve a common goal? Or perhaps all of these plus something else?

Understanding what is inside of the *black box* of collective leadership is of key importance. If we do not know what we are learning how can we know how to learn it? What is perhaps even more challenging is how the Team Coaches, not knowing what leadership is themselves, can support their students in that learning.

The purpose of this chapter article is not to provide an answer to what the exact form of leadership is but rather offer some thought for consideration. One approach which might be particularly helpful is the so-called DAC theory of outcomes (Drath et al., 2008). The core of DAC framework is its three strands: direction, alignment, and commitment. These three are suggested as key artefacts generated by leadership understood as a collective process. Direction describes the collective agreement on overall goals. Alignment refers to the co-ordination of work and knowledge within the group. Commitment refers to mutual responsibility for the team (McCauley & Fick-Cooper, 2020).

The outcome theory of leadership is not only simple and easy to understand but also seems very practical. It might be used to measure and assess the effectiveness of the group's leadership process, as well as help to locate the area of difficulties.

The Team Coach, using the DAC frameworks as a tool of support, can offer the team they work with the following questions:

- How well is this team united in a common direction?
- How well is the work of this team aligned across its members?
- Are members of this team giving the effort needed for the team to succeed? How many people are dedicated to this team?

(adapted from McCauley & Fick-Cooper, 2020).

On the Team Academy-based programmes leadership is both learned passively (e.g. students are asked to attend workshop/seminar and read on the subject) but also experienced *on the job* with learners provided with opportunities to engage and participate in the process of leadership in a variety of contexts and settings. The key component of effective learning is a reflection which again is a tool commonly used across Team Academy-based programmes. Reflection allows students to analyse, understand, and assimilate their experience (Boud et al., 2013).

On the Team Academy programmes, reflections happen through written and oral assignments, as well as during 1-2-1 coaching meetings, feedback given at the end of each training sessions, in the form of so-called *Post Motorolas* or *Post Project Reviews* (these are used for reviewing learning on projects both before the project takes place and after) and finally *360 feedback session* where students give views on themselves, others and processes they experienced. It is important to note reflection does not have to be used as a tool for learning from the past (i.e. *looking back* and analysing experiences which already took place). Scharmer (2009) suggested we can use reflection as a tool of envisioning the future we desire. Again, this is where the role of the Team Coaches is so important. The Team Coach, using that future-orientated approach can support student learning *when it happens* to guide the team to achieve the outcomes which matter. The following questions can be used as guidance:

- How the process we are experiencing right now moves this team towards the direction this team desires?
- Is the coordination of work as we experience it right now, the coordination that the team needs?
- What impact the combined current levels of commitment of the each of the team members will create for the future of this team?

In the following section, a summary of key observations as discussed so far is offered together with potential learning outcomes.

Key Observation 1

- Numerous leadership theories interplay with each other at once in any given team. It might be helpful if Team Coaches have an understanding of these theories to be able to more effectively support the team members with capturing leadership learning.
  Suggested leadership related learning outcome

- Students can recognize, discuss, and evaluate the leadership(s) theories applied in their team/projects.

## Key Observation 2

- The interaction between leaders and followers is in constant flux. These roles are never static (one is never only a leader or only a follower) but interplay with each other, shifting moment by moment.
  Suggested leadership related learning outcome:

  - Students can provide and discuss examples of leadership situations with them acting both as a leader and a follower.

## Key Observation 3

- Leadership is a collective process happening between individuals.
  Suggested leadership related learning outcome:

  - Students can describe leadership as a "process" which emerges shaped by all team members and develops across time.

## Key Observation 4

- Generating and sustaining *collective responsibility* seems a key struggle of young entrepreneurs. The challenge for Team Academy-based programmes is to support students in addressing this obstacle effectively, encouraging perseverance in learning and continuation of experimenting with the leadership process.
  Suggested leadership related learning outcome:

  - Students are able to review to what extent the concept of *collective responsibility* impacts the effectiveness of the leadership process in the teams they are members of.

## Key Observation 5

- There is no *right* or *wrong* way of learning collective leadership. Even *one-person* entrepreneurs can be supported in gaining a clear understanding of the concept. The role of the Team Coach is to underline the importance of acquiring the skill of collective leadership when allowing students to find their own ways of learning and practising the skill.

Suggested leadership related learning outcome:

- Students can recognize how they practise learning collective leadership.

Key Observation 6:

- The key to learning leadership is the reflection which allows students to monitor their evolving leadership engagement. The Team Coach might use reflection to harvest learning based on the past experiences as well as a tool of intervention to support students in creating the leadership process they desire when that process is just about to emerge. The outcome theory of leadership might be used to help the Team Coach formulate questions to further support students in that process.

Suggested leadership related learning outcome:

- Students can demonstrate their ability to use reflection to learn from the past experience as well as use reflection to shape the leadership processes as they emerge.

## Conclusions

This article focused on exploring leadership as a collective process. The aim was to bring more clarity about the concept of collective leadership, and to start a dialogue on the topic so that further perspectives and observations could be shared, gathered, and discussed. Numerous theories have been introduced and these were then applied to the context of the Team Academy programmes. The key observations had been shared together with suggested leadership related learning outcomes. These included complexity of collective leadership (including the simultaneous interplay of various theories), collective leadership being inseparable part of team existence, or usefulness of grasping the intangibility of collective leadership by e.g. focusing on the level of outcomes it generates (e.g. direction, alignment, and commitment).

Future research could further explore each of these, and, for example, study which of the collective leadership theories occur most predominantly in the environment of Team Academy programmes.

It is hoped the chapter inspires, challenges, and questions not only the concept of collective leadership itself but also how it manifests itself in the context of the Team Academy programmes.

## References

Antonacopoulou, E. P., & Bento, R. F. (2004). Methods of 'learning leadership': Taught and experiential. *Leadership in Organizations: Current Issues and Key Trends* (pp. 81–102). London: Routledge.

Baker, S. D. (2007). Followership: The theoretical foundation of a contemporary construct. *Journal of Leadership & Organizational Studies, 14*(1), 50–60.

Baldwin, C., & Linnea, A. (2010). *The circle way: A leader in every chair.* Oakland, CA: Berrett-Koehler Publishers.

Boud, D., Keogh, R., & Walker, D. (Eds). (2013). *Reflection: Turning experience into learning.* London: Routledge.

Carter, D. R., & Dechurch, L. A. (2012). Networks: The way forward for collectivistic leadership research. *Industrial and Organizational Psychology, 5*(4), 412.

Ciulla, J. B. (1995). Leadership ethics: Mapping the territory. *Business Ethics Quarterly, 5*(1), 5–28.

Conger, J. A. (2004). Developing leadership capability: What's inside the black box?. *Academy of Management Perspectives, 18*(3), 136–139.

DeRue, D. S., Nahrgang, J. D., Wellman, N. E. D., & Humphrey, S. E. (2011). Trait and behavioral theories of leadership: An integration and meta-analytic test of their relative validity. *Personnel Psychology, 64*(1), 7–52.

D'Intino, R. S., Goldsby, M. G., Houghton, J. D., & Neck, C. P. (2007). Self-leadership: A process for entrepreneurial success. *Journal of Leadership & Organizational Studies, 13*(4), 105–120.

Drath, W. H., McCauley, C. D., Palus, C. J., Van Velsor, E., O'Connor, P. M., & McGuire, J. B. (2008). Direction, alignment, commitment: Toward a more integrative ontology of leadership. *The Leadership Quarterly, 19*(6), 635–653.

García-Morales, V. J., Llorens-Montes, F. J., & Verdú-Jover, A. J. (2006). Antecedents and consequences of organizational innovation and organizational learning in entrepreneurship. *Industrial Management & Data Systems, 19*(4).

Holmberg-Wright, K., & Hribar, T. (2016). Soft skills-the missing piece for entrepreneurs to grow a business. *American Journal of Management, 16*(1), 11.

Isaacs, W. (1999). *Dialogue and the art of thinking together: A pioneering approach to communicating in business and in life.* NYC: Broadway Business.

Lord, R. G., & Hall, R. J. (2005). Identity, deep structure and the development of leadership skill. *The Leadership Quarterly, 16*(4), 591–615.

McCauley, C., & Fick-Cooper, L. (2020). *Direction, alignment, commitment: Achieving better results through leadership.* Center for Creative Leadership.

Pearce, C. L., & Conger, J. A. (2002). *Shared leadership: Reframing the hows and whys of leadership*. London: Sage Publications.

Porter, L. W., & McLaughlin, G. B. (2006). Leadership and the organizational context: like the weather? *The Leadership Quarterly, 17*(6), 559–576.

Scharmer, C. O. (2009). *Theory U: Learning from the future as it emerges*. Oakland, CA: Berrett-Koehler Publishers.

Spillane, J. P. (2005). Distributed leadership. In *The educational forum* (Vol. 69, No. 2, pp. 143–150). Germantown, NY: Taylor & Francis Group.

Stogdill, R. M., & Shartle, C. L. (1948). Methods for determining patterns of leadership behavior in relation to organization structure and objectives. *Journal of Applied Psychology, 32*(3), 286.

Uhl-Bien, M., Marion, R., & McKelvey, B. (2007). Complexity leadership theory: Shifting leadership from the industrial age to the knowledge era. *The Leadership Quarterly, 18*(4), 298–318.

Yammarino, F. J., Salas, E., Serban, A., Shirreffs, K., & Shuffler, M. L. (2012). Collectivistic leadership approaches: Putting the "we" in leadership science and practice. *Industrial and Organizational Psychology, 5*(4), 382–402.

Zaccaro, S. J., Rittman, A. L., & Marks, M. A. (2001). Team leadership. *The Leadership Quarterly, 12*(4), 451–483.

# 6 Fitting My Own Oxygen Mask: On the Challenges of Leading the Self as a Team Coach

*Elinor Vettraino*

## Introduction

As I write this chapter, some months after I technically should have, the irony of my area of focus is not lost on me. Self-leadership and I have been somewhat uncomfortable bedfellows throughout my life, although interestingly not consistently. There are particular times where I find the draw of what I *should* do is far less appealing that the possibility of what I *could* do. And so, I find myself at the eleventh-hour, attempting to draw together my ideas, beliefs, experiences, and provocations around how I, and other coaches, lead ourselves through the lived experiences of a Team Academy (TA)[1] programme. This somewhat autoethnographic chapter, therefore, explores how I have experienced and been challenged by self-leadership as a coach within the TA model, what reflections I have on moments of challenge and ways forward, and offers some potential provocations for future thinking.

## Self-leadership

Unlike the broader concept of leadership, self-leadership has a relatively clear definition which sees the concept as a process, embedding cognitive and behavioural strategies to enable individuals to positively control and influence their own lives (Neck & Houghton, 2006; Manz & Neck, 2004, Houghton et al., 2003). The concept of self-leadership originated from discourse in the 1980s and 1990s focused on concepts such as self-management and self-regulation (Carver & Scheier, 1981; Manz & Neck, 1999), and as a concept it has faced criticism primarily relating to the similarities that exist between it and theories relating to psychological constructs of identity or conscientiousness. However, self-leadership differs from both self-management and self-regulation

DOI: 10.4324/9781003163121-6

because although these concepts explore people's behaviour, with one being more prescriptive (self-management) than the other (self-regulation), neither consider the types of, or rationale for, the behaviours people engage in and offer insight into how one might affect change. This latter point is important to note. Understanding how and why we might choose to move towards, or avoid, activities and experiences help to shape our way of engaging with the world. However, identifying what lies beneath our approach to experiences requires honest and critical self-reflection and that can create moments of anxiety that strike at the heart of an individual.

Let us return to the strategies that individuals can employ to support their self-leadership. These are generally grouped into three areas: behaviour focused, strategies focused on developing natural rewards, and cognitive strategies (Neck & Houghton, 2006). Strategies focused on behaviour are about raising self-awareness of how and when an individual behaves in a particular way and then using techniques such as creative goal setting or positive affirmations as a way of channelling behaviour to enhance personal performance. Interestingly, Neck and Houghton (2006) highlight self-awareness relating to tasks that might be seen as unpleasant but important to do and pose the question of what behaviours occur at this point and why. Drawing attention to how we react at times when we really don't want to do something can enable the individual to see patterns in their actions and then create a break in the cycle of behaviours, akin to the idea of creating a *stop* moment (Appelbaum, 1995; Fels, 1998, 2012, 2015).

When we consider natural rewards as a strategy for self-leadership, these can be trickier to find because they are the intrinsic motivators that exist in carrying out a particular task. Suggestions to enhance this strategic approach would be to attempt to find ways to incorporate more enjoyment into particular tasks, thereby increasing the likelihood of wanting to engage (Manz & Neck, 2004). Another potential approach would be to refocus attention and energy into the aspects of the task that might be more pleasant, thereby increasing engagement with the more enjoyable elements of the activity (Manz & Sims, 2001). Thinking back to how you might do this when a task is inherently unpleasant to an individual provides an interesting challenge here, and perhaps a way of working through this aligns with the third strategy grouping suggested; that of cognitive reframing.

Self-leadership can falter when we focus our energy on negative thinking. Boal (1995) calls these negative thought patterns *cops in the head*, a reference to being held in check by our own thought processes and the stories that we tell ourselves about our self-efficacy. Cognitive reframing helps to create constructive thought processes and patterns that move thinking away from limiting beliefs or assumptions. By doing so, our thought processes challenge potentially dysfunctional or unhelpful ways of viewing our world that can often be based on irrational beliefs, and instead create patterns of thinking that enable us to view experiences through a more constructive lens.

## *A Little Story of Self-sabotage*

In 2016, I *finally* succeeded in completing my doctorate. This was an 8-year epic saga worthy of folklore during which I encountered all manner of challenges; real and imagined, externally created and internally held. Out of all of the obstacles that I found to put in the way of my own success, lack of effective self-leadership was arguably the most critical. Curiously, I was perfectly capable of leading myself effectively in most situations; I had challenging jobs during this period of time, changed organizations twice, dealt with significant health issues along with bereavement. Through all of those, I managed to keep doing *the day job* and function creatively and effectively. When it came to reading for or writing up my doctoral work however, completely different story. I always seemed to find something more important to do like cleaning the house, going for a run, doing more of the day job than required. I even published a book with a colleague about my doctoral work (Vettraino & Linds, 2015) while not actually doing my doctoral work.

What was going on with my self-leadership?

2015 was a tipping point for me because I was nearly out of time to complete, and yet I felt incapable of doing what needed to be done. A chance conversation with a new colleague turned that situation around and reflecting on what made such a transformation in my process highlighted to me what had been holding me back. Essentially, I was filled with self-doubt about my academic capability. I had been told as a child that I was *the artistic one* in the family and should leave the academic *stuff* to my siblings. As a result, I carried this negative belief about my academic prowess throughout my school, college, and then university years; the latter as both a student and later an academic staff member. Tracking back now in my behaviours, I can see the kind of distorted thinking patterns emerging, akin to imposter syndrome, not uncommon in academic life (Bothello & Roulet, 2019); the very patterns that self-leadership strategies are designed to overturn. I wrote off my successes because academically I *obviously* wasn't capable so there must be another reason, right?

I finally stopped doing this when I successfully defended my viva.

Interestingly, that wasn't because I had finally completed my doctorate. It was because I had derailed my thought pattern, I had truly stopped to sit in the moment of discomfort about my capability and instead consider what had changed in me to enable me to succeed. It was a reflexive experience, a moment of thoughtful action that created the chance to flex, bend back (the literal meaning of the etymological root of reflexive), to see around and beyond what was in front of me (Steier, 1991). I had challenged my long-held assumptions and found them to be baseless and as a result, I had been able to navigate out of a repeating and negative holding pattern.

The connection between this experience and my current situation as a team coach lies in understanding how I lead myself; as a learner and now as the programme lead for team entrepreneurship programmes, and as a team coach. The behaviours, attitudes, and practices that I engage in at moments of real challenge for me need to be explored, along with how they can positively or negatively impact on my leadership of self. And, to understand that more fully, we need to briefly explore how team coaching manifests in the context of TA. Coaching in educational contexts is therefore where we turn next.

## Team Coaching in the Context of TA

As a relatively new discipline in the coaching world, team coaching has gained traction in the last decade, and there is still debate as to what team coaching is and how it differs from other forms of coaching processes (Widdowson & Barbour, 2021). A number of definitions have been posited which indicate the particular importance of collaborative performance, a common goal, collective capability, and the ability to think systemically about the work that occurs in and around the team (Hawkins & Turner, 2019; Thornton, 2010). In the last year, Widdowson and Barbour (2021) produced a further helpful definition in their text on team coaching that considers it to be about helping *"teams work together, with others and within their wider environment, to create lasting change … [and] better ways of working and new thinking"* (p. 8). In relation to TA specifically, Fowle and Jussila (2016) state in their paper on TA, *"coaching sessions, or training sessions as they are called in Finland, are at the heart of the Team Academy model"* (p. 2). Team coaching in a TA context is about all of the elements of Widdowson and Barbour's definition; collective and collaborative understanding that moves the team beyond the confines of their own micro-world and enables them to think more broadly about the impact of their ways of being, doing and thinking on the world so that they may affect positive and productive change. However, the context of operating in an educational programme needs to be considered.

Unlike traditional programmes of study, certainly in the UK, the coaching approach to delivery of learning moves the experience far away from the *push* approach to education, and instead encourages a *pull* model of learning. In the former, the student is very much a *passive recipient* of information, with the lecturer or tutor being the expert who delivers (or *pushes*) the knowledge into the student normally through lecture or seminar-based experiences. In the latter, the student is instead an *active participant* in the learning process, proactively co-creating and, in the case of TA, self-determining the direction of their learning experience and developing subject competence as a result. The coach in the TA model effectively *pulls* the learning from the student through active listening and supportive challenge, provocation through questioning and support for them and their team as they hold each other to account.

Specifically related to team coaching in the TA model, in his seminal text, Partanen (2012) put forward his *theses of team coaching* which summarizes the core of the ethos behind the TA coaching approach. Included in this are the following:

- The importance of the team coach's personality, which Partanen suggests is the *most important tool* for a coach.
- The impact of dialogue in a team. Based on the work of Bohm (1991, 1996) and Isaacs (1999), Partanen suggests that dialogue is the lifeblood of the team's process.
- The challenge and benefit of diversity in a team. In line with Belbin's (1993) work on team roles, Partanen suggests that differences in a team are a core resource for success.
- The benefit of conflict in a team as an opportunity for growth and development.
- The laws of intervention and non-intervention; summarized as intervene when you think you shouldn't, don't intervene when you think you should.

Partanen's ideas of the team coach's approach and role are useful to consider in relation to how learning is *delivered* in traditional programmes of study, and in particular with the contrasting expectations of different pedagogical approaches. It is in the philosophy of these contrasting approaches that the first point of discomfort can be found for me.

## Square Peg, Round Hole

The reason for my discomfort lies in the context within which most TA programmes tend to operate, certainly in the UK. Unlike the kind of corporate coaching contexts inferred, or explicitly referred to, by Widdowson and Barbour (2021), the TA model attempts to offer team coaching as the model of delivery for Higher Education (HE) level programmes of study. In the UK, these programmes are situated in heavily bureaucratic organizations that are less likely or able to embrace the emergent and client-led approach more commonly experienced through coaching. Increasingly measured on the quality of the outcome for students (employability, quality of experience), as well as the output (quality of degree), these institutions can struggle to support the development of the culture that is required to enable such innovative pedagogies to flourish. This is particularly important in the early days of programmes where both the student and coaching teams are learning together to establish the approach.

The way in which learning occurs in the TA model creates challenges for many traditional educators because it requires the staff member to step back and allow the learner to lead. As already highlighted, in traditional programmes of study, a lecturer or teacher gives some form of input, normally in lecture or workshop-based experiences. Some form of self-directed work might form part of the learning process, with students engaging potentially in group activities that are then fed back to the broader cohort in a plenary session. In the TA model, learning is *delivered* through engagement in activities such as dialogue, suggested by Partanen earlier, in coached sessions involving teams of learners (known as Team Entrepreneurs or Teampreneurs – TEs) rather than groups of individuals. The team coach's role is not to be an expert voice in the room, but rather to hold the space for collective reflection, developmental discussion, and the generation of communal action. There is an expectation that the TEs themselves lead the learning process, adopting a heutagogical approach to their progression through subject competence development (Blaschke & Hase, 2016). This self-determined approach to learning is scaffolded through the same elements that support a traditional programme; the module framework that indicates core learning to be achieved. What is different in a TA programme is that the way in which the learning occurs, the timing of it, and the process used are all directed by the TEs, supported by the team coach.

Cycling back to the reason for my point of discomfort, as the academic *keeper* of the TA model in my institution, I am constantly balancing the tension between the slow, emergent, and socially constructed learning processes evident in the TA model, and the need for robust and valid evidence of learning through typical academic structures such as assessment and feedback loops. With the COVID challenges this year, my anxiety here manifested as concern, among other things, about the lack of appropriate business activity for many of our learners. I could see the frustration in many of our TEs who found conceptualizing virtual value creation as almost impossible. The lack of embodied connection with their colleagues and teammates also made the process of learning from the work of others much harder, and for some, it was unachievable. How, then, do we assess the business of doing business, when there was no business being done? The academic standards for the programme quite rightly dictate that our learners must be subject to the same robust standards as any other student undertaking an equivalent level of programme. Our assessment process, our moderation, our approach to marking and professional dialogue relating to this was clear and thorough, and yet I created additional assessment sessions, 1-1s, team coaches' meetings, all to assuage my own anxiety about our approach; was it enough? This was arguably good professional practice but I am aware that it was driven by my reaction rather than our coaching team's proaction. I feel I was being led through this process by my anxiety rather than through reflective or reflexive processes.

Connected with the challenge of activity in our TEs was another area of difficulty, that of their readiness to learn.

## The Light Is On, the Door Is Open But I'm Just Not Ready

In most cases, those who are making the transition into TA programmes at university are young adults, leaving home for the first time. They have to manage themselves through the complexity of relocating physically to a place they may never have actually been to or have only been to once or twice for open day type activities. On top of geographically navigating their way, they have to relocate their mental, emotional, and academic selves creating challenges for them around readiness to learn and self-leadership; neither of which are that straightforward for many 18-year olds.

COVID has added exponentially to the challenges associated with being ready to learn. At a time when most first-year students would be beginning the rite of passage into friendship formations and social activities, our TEs found themselves facing the same four walls of their family bedroom or possibly their room in halls of residence, unable to meet others, share experiences and begin the journey of learning-by-doing in a physical space. This impacted heavily upon their sense of competence in engaging in entrepreneurial action, and their sense of identity as a TE and their commitment to being part of their team and the wider TA community.

Tait (2000, p. 289) describes *"essential and interdependent"* support functions that need to be in place for students making the transition into university education; these are focused on:

- Cognitive support – developing students' learning and understanding through the standard kinds of course materials and resources that programmes of study at HE use.
- Affective support – creating a nurturing and supportive environment for the students that addresses welfare and pastoral needs and makes them feel welcome and at ease.
- Systems support – having appropriate, open, and effective administrative systems and processes/procedures in place.

Tait was contextualizing these functions in relation to distance-learning students. The impact of COVID on our working practices as team coaches this year meant that to all intents and purposes, our TEs *were* distance-learning students. As with all educational establishments around the world, we pivoted swiftly, and systems began to be in place to support the TEs' progress through the academic functions of the course. Addressing their cognitive needs was also something that the coaching team worked hard to do, and, based on the feedback from the TEs, we provided additional elements of structure that are more commonly found in traditional educational programmes. Interestingly, this provides a second point of discomfort for me as a coach. What created the need to add in this level of structure? The TEs asked for more scaffolding but did I respond because of my anxiety as a team coach and the academic responsible for the programme as discussed earlier, or because it was truly beneficial to the TEs? Whose need did the response serve? Did I *discount* the *Law of Intervention* (Partanen, 2012)?

The affective support was much harder for us to develop effectively, particularly in line with the overarching philosophy of the model which is that of developing a community of practice. The novelty of virtual coaching sessions wore off around June 2020 with our then second years, and by January 2021, our first years and masters level TEs were also jaded and worn out by a sense of stagnation and inaction. We built in monthly 1-1 coaching sessions, developed community learning sessions, and created a virtual *open-door* approach to contact. We were much more proactive in terms of reaching out to the TEs individually and collectively and that seemed to support the sense of being part of a community. However, it was in the moments where we were able to physically gather (socially distanced and appropriately masked) with one of a team, that the sense of connection was explicitly clear. Both the coaching team and some of the TEs put time and energy into thinking through how and why these connections would take place. As Parker said in her game-changing text *The Art of the Gathering*: *"Gatherings crackle and flourish when real thought goes into them, when (often invisible) structure is baked into them, and when a host has the curiosity, willingness, and generosity of spirit to try"* (2018, p. xiv).

And here is where I felt the third point of discomfort. I recognized my own growing anxiety about the way in which some of the TEs were disconnecting not just from the programme, but more importantly from each other. This disconnection changed the way in which each TE thought about themselves and their place within the team and the community. Indeed, were they in teams at all, never mind a community?

## *Building a Community of Practice in a Pandemic*

When TEs join a TA programme, they are not (often) ready-made effective and high performing team players, able to understand their place in the bigger system of teams. In fact, Thornton's (2010) suggestion that *"all teams are groups, but not all groups are teams"* (p. 34) is as true for TEs as it is for any other student cohort in the early stages of a programme of study. Regarding TEs within a programme as being within a community of practice is a natural consideration when viewing the definition of such. Wenger et al. define communities of practice as *"groups of people who share a concern, a set of problems, or a passion about a topic, and who deepen their knowledge and expertise in this area by interacting on an ongoing basis"* (p. 7). While not always being through choice – often TEs are initially formed into *groups* at the beginning of their programmes in order to facilitate manageable numbers for team coaches to work with – the focus for the community formation with the TEs is to enable them to create value through a shared and socially constructed process. By forming groups which become teams, the TEs are creating new knowledge from the connection with others; what McNamee (2004) would regard as *during and with*, as opposed to learning individually *after and from* (Creswell, 2007).

However, the approach to learning in the UK tends towards a much more individualistic way of thinking, something which has become exacerbated by COVID. Individualism can be defined as *"a situation where people are concerned with themselves and close family members only"* (Abdel-Fattah et al., 2003, p. 47) and quite understandably, many of our TEs became consumed by their own and their family's health and wellbeing. TEs manifesting mental ill-health became much more prevalent and rather than feeling as though they could draw on the strength of the team, they in fact became more isolated and introspective. My reaction was to provoke more connection and to proactively engage those TEs who were willing in activities and events that would stimulate some form of team response. Some of these activities worked well but in doing so, I was struck by similar questions to my earlier points of discomfort: whose need does this serve? Whose anxiety am I responding to, mine or theirs? The duality of the roles I have to embody plays a part in this questioning because as a Programme Director I am responsible for the output of the courses I lead, and my choices around activities I engage the TEs in (or attempt to engage them in) are therefore restricted by the requirements of that role. And on the other hand, I am a team coach, I am there at the service of the team and what I do reflects my attempts to support their learning, cohesion, sense of connection, and ability to *do* as well as *be*.

## Reflections on Dealing with Discomfort

You might notice a pattern here. A repetition of anxiety, followed by action, followed by questions. Although the questions always focus on the needs of the TEs and my anxiety around that, essentially at the root of the questions is always the same fear; am I capable? Confidence is a core component of being a coach, according to Widdowson and Barbour (2021). Not to be confused with arrogance, this sense of *being* confident is about valuing what I as a coach bring to the table, while also being able to be open enough to show vulnerability. I liken this to the concept of negative capability, the ability to sit with discomfort and use it as a way of understanding how to move productively, albeit potentially slowly, forward. This concept has been explored in relation to leadership development (French, 2001; Jameson, 2012; Saggurthi & Thakur, 2015; Simpson & French, 2006) and is therefore appropriate to consider here. Leading the self requires the ability to harness both the cognitive and affective domains which can often wrestle with each other. Being comfortable with uncertainty and ambiguity is what we aim to foster in our TEs, so my ability to *"tolerate anxiety and fear, to stay in the place of uncertainty in order to allow for the emergence of new thoughts or perceptions"* (Eisold, 2000, p. 65) is important to cultivate and I offer some reflections below on how my work-in-progress is developing.

## Get over Yourself!

I am reminded as I read this of Tilda Swinton's character in Marvel's *Dr Strange* essentially telling the hero to *get over yourself!* I don't believe I am alone in having a tendency as a coach to feel that if something is not working it must be because of something I am doing or not doing rather than believing that maybe it's nothing to do with me, maybe it's about what the TEs are doing, or the fact that it's a Wednesday, or that the world is in the grip of a global pandemic. A great reminder of this occurred recently when one of my TEs wrote as a reflection on an activity he was hosting in his end of year portfolio, words to the effect of *thank you Elinor for letting me host this session because you don't always leave me the space to do that.* Having recovered from the initial embarrassment of realizing that this year in particular I have had a tendency to be more *present* than is always helpful(!), I learned a valuable lesson in slowing the reflective process down. In the session the TE was discussing, I had made a conscious effort to be wholly present in the moment, sit with concerns I had about how the session would go, or who should be doing what. The concept of patience in this respect is key. As Simpson and French (2006) indicate, patience in this regard is not about inaction, it is instead about achieving *considered* action which comes from taking a conscious time out. Appelbaum (1995) would refer to this as a *stop* moment; *"the advent of intelligent choice"* (p. xiv). This in turn leads me to another reflection.

## Considering the Laws of Intervention and Non-intervention (Partanen, 2012)

Learning how to navigate the role of team coach as an academic requires the ability to engage in an iterative and organic self-reflexive process. Drawing from my theatre roots, I would term this reflexive dance *metaxis* (Boal, 1995). Belonging in two worlds; that of the reality that is experienced through the senses, and that which is embodied and internal, metaxis asks both the actor (the person) and the character (the role they play, the team coach) to engage in a dialogue of practice. At times, this dialogue is externalized through interventions with the coached team, at other times, the wrestle takes place behind the scenes. That doesn't mean that intervention doesn't take place; many team coaches (myself included) find it hard not to allow our emotions to show in our faces, on our bodies. Partanen's (2012) view is that personality is key in the coaching process and I would argue this is supported by Widdowson and Barbour's (2021) suggestion that courage is a key part of *being* a team coach. For them, it follows that a team coach will respond in the moment and have the *"courage to use how you are feeling in the moment ... becoming comfortable with discomfort"* (authors' emphasis, p. 37).b

I have learned over the years, but particularly in this last year, that when I am mindful of *"responding instead of reacting"* (Widdowson & Barbour, 2021, p. 38) and staying present with the team, I am most effective. Focusing on reflexive writing during the session has enabled me to develop this further and noticing my discomfort has enabled me (more often than not) to let it go. According to Widdowson and Barbour (2021), understanding the gift that I bring to the table is important, whilst also being open to accepting when I am unsure or at a loss. Lawrence and Whyte (cited in Widdowson & Barbour, 2021) also highlight the reality that coaches become comfortable with feeling a lack of confidence or capability. So, accepting that these feelings are an important part of my growth as a coach.

## Provocations and Closure

The writing of this chapter has enabled me to put into words a few of the challenges I have faced as a team coach in attempting to lead myself productively and for the good of those I coach. It has also offered me the chance to consider prompts for my future practice that I share with you in closing, with the intention of perhaps provoking further reflection in your own practice:

*Learning to let go* – I cannot always square the purpose I have as a team coach with that of a Programme Director. Learning to let go of the anxiety around these two sometimes disparate roles is an important, and yet challenging, requirement if I am to bring my best self to either.

*I am responsible only for myself* – this is an approach I have often shared with friends, colleagues and clients, and yet I have a tendency to take responsibility for others in a way that is neither helpful to them, nor beneficial to me or the task at hand.

*Noticing when anxiety surfaces* – it is not always easy in the moment to realize when anxiety is creating action but there are markers that can help. Writing from a psychoanalytical perspective, Eisold (2000) identifies *"humour, confusion, confrontation"* (p. 65) as useful potential cues, and I certainly recognize the first two in my behaviours when not at my best. It is at these moments when my final provocation becomes essential.

*Take the time* – finally, critical self-reflection is a core part of effective self-leadership. In times of crisis and challenge, it is all too easy to say *I have no time* for these activities and yet they are a core part of ensuring best practice. Taking a step back from an experience and considering why, what, and how it occurred, as well as my place in it, enables distanced analysis of action and creates the potential for growth and change (Eisold, 2000)

## Note

1 The Team Academy (TA) model (and programmes) referred to in this chapter is the model of entrepreneurship education first generated in Jyväskylä, Finland in 1993 by Johannes Partanen. The model has, at its core, the central principles of learning in teams and learning-by-doing. Students on TA-based programmes (known as Team Entrepreneurs or Teampreneurs – TEs) and normally in universities or higher education institutions, work in teams throughout the duration of their programme, to set up and run real money-making organizations through which they learn about business and entrepreneurship. A fundamental tenant of the model is that there is no formalized teaching in the model; instead, the teams of learners are coached by a team coach through the successes and challenges of working with others towards the creation of a common goal. There have been a number of articles and texts explaining the core model; however, the original concept can be read about in Partanen's seminal text *The team coach's best tools* (2017).

## References

Abdel-Fattah, E. D., & Huber, G. L. (2003). Individualism vs. collectivism in different cultures: A cross-cultural study. *Intercultural Education, 14*(1), 47–56. doi:10.1080/1467598032000044647.

Appelbaum, D. (1995). *The stop.* Albany: State University of New York Press.

Belbin, M. (1993). *Team roles at work.* London: Routledge.

Boal, A. (1995). *The rainbow of desire: Boal's method of theatre and therapy.* Translated from Portuguese by A. Jackson. London: Routledge.

Blaschke, L. M., & Hase, S. (2016). Heutagogy: A holistic framework for creating 21st century self-determined learners. In B. Gros & M. Maina Kinshuk (Eds), *The future of ubiquitous learning: Learning designs for emerging pedagogies* (pp. 25–40), NYC: Springer.

Bohm, D. (1996). *On dialogue.* New York: Routledge.

Bohm, D., Factor, D., & Garrett, P. (1991). Dialogue – A proposal. http://www.david-bohm.net/dialogue/dialogue_proposal.html

Bothello, J., & Roulet, T. J. (2019). The imposter syndrome, or the misrepresentation of self in academic life. *Journal of Management Studies, 54*, 854–861. doi:10.1111/joms.12344.

Carver, C. S., & Scheier, M. F. (1981). *Attention and self-regulation: A control theory approach to human behaviour*. New York, NY: Springer-Verlag.

Creswell, J. (2007). *Qualitative inquiry and research design*, 2nd Edition. London: SAGE Publications.

Darwish, A-F. E., & Huber, G. L. (2003). Individualism vs collectivism in different cultures: A cross cultural study. *Intercultural Education, 14*(1), 47–55. doi:10.1080/1467598032000044647.

Derrickson, S. (2016). *Dr Strange*. Motion Picture.

Eisold, K. (2000). The rediscovery of the unknown: An inquiry into psycho-analytic practice. *Contemporary Psychoanalysis, 36*(1), 57–75. doi:10.1080/00107530.2000.10747045

Fels, L. (1998). In the wind, clothes on a dance line. *Journal of Curriculum Theorizing, 14*(1), 27–36.

Fels, L. (2012). Collecting data through performative inquiry: A tug on the sleeve. *Youth Theatre Journal, 26*(1), 50–60. doi:10.1080/08929092.2012.678209.

Fels, L. (2015). Performative inquiry: Reflection as a scholarly pedagogical act. In E. Vettraino & W. Linds (Eds), *Playing in a house of mirrors: Applied theatre as reflective practice* (pp. 151–174). Rotterdam: Sense Publishers.

Fowle, M., & Jussila, N. (2016). Team Academy: The adoption of a Finnish learning model in the UK. *Conference proceedings: 11th European Conference on Innovation and Entrepreneurship (ECIE)*.

French, R. (2001). "Negative capability": Managing the confusing un-certainties of change. *Journal of Organisational Change Management, 14*(5), 480–492. doi:10.1108/EUM0000000005876.

Hawkins, P., & Turner, E. (2019). *Systemic coaching: Delivering value beyond the individual*. London: Routledge.

Houghton, J., Neck, C. P., & Manz, C. C. (2003). Self leadership and super leadership: The heart and the art of creating shared leadership in teams. In C. L. Pearce & J. A. Conger (Eds), *Shared leadership: Reframing the hows and whys of leadership* (pp. 123–140). Thousand Oaks, CA: SAGE Publications.

Isaacs, W. (1999). *Dialogue: The art of thinking together*. New York: Bantam Doubleday.

Jameson, J. (2012). Leadership, values, trust and negative capability: Managing the uncertainties of future English higher education. *Higher Education Quarterly, 66*(4), 391–414. doi:10.1111/j.1468-2273.2012.00533.x.

Manz, C. C., & Neck, C. P. (1999). *Mastering self-leadership: Empowering yourself for personal excellence*, 2nd Edition. Upper Saddle River, NJ: Prentice-Hall.

Manz, C. C., & Neck, C. P. (2004). *Mastering self-leadership: Empowering yourself for personal excellence*, 3rd Edition. Upper Saddle River, NJ: Pearson Prentice-Hall.

Manz, C. C., & Sims, H. P. Jr. (2001). *New superleadership: Leading others to lead themselves*. San Francisco, CA: Berrett-Koehler.

McNamee, S. (2004). Relational bridges between constructionism and constructivism. In J. D. Raskin & S. K. Bridges (Eds), *Studies in meaning 2: Bridging the personal and the social in constructivist psychology* (pp. 37–50). NYC: Pace University Press.

Neck, C. P., & Houghton, J. (2006). Two decades of self-leadership theory and research: Past developments, present trends, future possibilities. *Journal of Managerial Psychology, 21*(4), 270–295. doi: 10.1108/02683940610663097.

Parker, P. (2018). *The art of gathering: How we meet and why it matters.* London: Penguin Books.

Partanen, J. (2012). *The team coach's best tools.* Jyväskylä, Finland: Partus.

Saggurthi, S., & Thakur (2015). Usefulness of uselessness: A case for negative capability in management. *Academy of Management Learning & Education, 15*(1), 180–193. doi: 10.5465/amle.2013.0250.

Simpson, P., & French, R. (2006). Negative capability and the capacity to think in the present moment. *Leadership, 2*(2), 245–255. doi: 10.1177/1742 71500606293.

Steier, F. (1991). *Research and reflexivity.* London: SAGE Publications.

Tait, A. (2000). Planning student support for open and distance learning. *Open Learning, 15*(3), 287–299.

Thornton, C. (2010). *Group and team coaching: The essential guide.* London: Routledge.

Vettraino, E., & Linds, W. (2015). *Playing in a house of mirrors: Applied theatre as reflective practice.* Rotterdam: Sense Publishers.

Wenger, E., McDermott, R. A., & Snyder, W. (2002). *Cultivating communities of practice: A guide to managing knowledge.* Harvard, MA: Harvard Business Press.

Widdowson, L., & Barbour, P. (2021). *Building top performing teams: A practical guide to team coaching to improve collaboration and drive organizational success.* London: Kogan Page.

# 7 The Influence of the Physical Working Environment on Employee Collaboration with a Highlight on Team Performance: Analysis of Coworking Sites in the Basque Country

*Amaia Aranceta Zubeldia,*
*Saioa Arando Lasagabaster, and*
*Izaskun Agirre Aranburu*

## Introduction

The concept of the physical working environment has become an extending area of research in recent years. Due to its prevalence for the analysis of work settings and its influence in the perspective and the understanding of current trends of work, the number of studies covering the physical and spatial aspects of work has considerably increased. Authors like Townsend et al. (1998) have spent years investigating the influence of changing workplaces on employees. Recently, many organizations have invested time and money in modifying the workplace to transversally improve other aspects of job performance like employee collaboration (Heerwagen et al., 2004; Sawyer, 2017). The world's biggest and most influential companies like Google[1] have also set a recurring trend of installing open office plans and encouraging teamwork and collaboration on the contrary to former and more traditional work settings. From standing prototyped offices with the same outline, structure, and design to more creative interiors like open areas, new trends in workplace design have affected the way we work. In addition, wireless technology has enabled us to work without being attached to one place at a time. According to Bender (2013), the technologically centred workspace has changed the understanding of space, as technology enables communication beyond

DOI: 10.4324/9781003163121-7

the physical distance. Workplaces have been reinvented to cover the needs of a changing reality technologically self-sufficient and independent, intended to satisfy the mobile nature of the current society. One of the examples of this form of changing workplaces and the changing nature of work is found at coworking spaces. In addition, the MTA, or Mondragon Team Academy,[2] is also set in an open space intended for teamwork and collaboration. A space without physical barriers has enabled MTA teams to share ideas and projects in an atmosphere of constant entrepreneurship and collaboration. As a leading laboratory for the Team Academy concept and structure, the space provides a physical environment suited for experimentation, innovation, and knowledge practices that lead the MTA into a worldwide reference.

## Collaboration and Team Performance as Effective Forms of the Socialization Process of Work Environments

Working groups function best when they have a shared identity and set common goals to succeed (Latham, 2007). On a day-to-day basis, collaboration marks the flow for setting common goals and working in partnership to achieve these goals. Schrage (1990) underlines the importance of collaboration and collaborative teams by narrating the different boundaries affected by collaborative processes in life. Furthermore, Vera (2000) highlights that human conditions like biological or cultural contribute to the socialization process as humans live in relation to others. Therefore, collaboration can be an innate attribute to human sociability, or extended to the concept that humans are sociable by nature. The need for socializing has sided groups and teams throughout history since Durkheim's mechanical solidarity as a fundamental component of status-groups. As Salas et al. (2017) state, a team is formed by two or more individuals that through interaction adopt specific roles while working towards shared goals. According to Salas et al. (2017), teams have a special nature as they are characterized by specific features only available in teams and in team performance like performing relevant tasks, social interaction, or the embodiment of an organizational context. Furthermore, according to authors like Hennemann et al. (1995, p. 44), one main requirement of collaboration is for the individuals participating in the collaborative process to feel themselves as members of the team, so it is intrinsic in the term and nature of collaboration that all participants in joint teamwork consider themselves as members of a team in a close feeling of membership and contribution. The physical working environment, otherwise, as the product of the socialization process at work settings according to Lefebvre (1905) should enable teamwork and collaboration through its positionality and functionality.

Workplaces, considering Lukacs, are the sites for the production and reproduction of life that goes beyond individual biological survival (Gianna, 2014) and for facilitating the space to enhance collaboration, it is essential to remodel the work environment by previously identifying spatial typologies that best influence collaboration and teamwork. Authors like Mattesisch and Monsey (2001) analysed and identified different factors affecting collaboration: 1 – Environment; 2 – Membership; 3 – Process and structure; 4 – Communication; 5 – Purpose; 6 – Resources. Teamwork marks the steps for achieving the factors listed by Mattesisch and Monsey (2001) as essential core processes to achieve collaboration. The suitability of the space for enabling teamwork will delimitate the type and amount of team working in a specific functional area. As Andriessen (2003) explains, the concept and nature of work is changing and so do the workers and their utensils as they overcome huge differences from former prospects.

As Foucault (1967) says, the individual lives in a space that rather than being empty, it is defined by a set of relations intrinsic to human nature. Coworking spaces, for example, have been created to facilitate job opportunities and to promote collaborative networks among their members. In the case of MTA space has also become an essential attribute for sustaining collaboration and the collaborative needs required for all members and students of the Team Academy. Inside the studying programme of leadership, entrepreneurship, and innovation (LEINN), Team Academy supposes a hiatus for experimentation, innovation, and student programmes that base their everyday methodology on teamwork and collaboration. These collaborative spaces as Becker (2004) explains are diverse places that accommodate the value of giving people lots of choice in where, when, and how they work. This way, the open-office design also characteristic of the MTA in the Faculty of Business of Mondragon, enables collaboration as it increases the possibility for casual interactions owing to the visibility of the space and the participating members. Likewise, the space has been transformed to fulfil the objectives set upon the spatial settings for enhancing teamwork and collaboration. Group cognitive processes are aimed for establishing teams and increasing collaboration for purposes covering the fulfilment of educational projects in the case of MTA, the integration of joint social projects for the community, or to find the synergy between teams and create active networks.

**Analysis**

The study has been divided into six stages: (i) the preliminary stage that includes a background analysis; (ii) the formulation of the problem that includes the hypotheses questions; (iii) the design of the research model; (iv) fieldwork, regarding the implementation of the survey, data collection, and data process; (v) the empirical analysis and the first results; (vi) main conclusions of the research.

*Sample*

Regarding the coworking space as the research unit of this study, the obtained sample of 10 makes around 35% of coworking spaces in the Basque Country. For conducting the empirical analysis, a survey has been shared between the workers of these spaces and 50 responses have been collected with more than one respondent for each of the analysed spaces. For that, a 7-point Likert scale has been used ranging from 1 – totally disagree – to 7 – totally agree.

*Method and Methodology*

This research project intends to measure variables in their natural state and as a result, the methodology used for the observation of the variables has been done through fieldwork. Consequently, it is preferable to use quantitative methodology as the use of this method to contrast hypotheses enables the researcher to have a global vision of the data collected and the results obtained. Besides, the quantitative method that aids the analysis of the causal relationships between variables is better justified for this study case due to the nature of data, which is numerical, and the hypotheses proposed. In addition, physical working environment indicators have been selected in relation to collaborative spaces taken from Hua et al. (2010) and Hua's own investigations (2010). Her investigation includes characteristics to measure the collaborative spatial features such as individual workstation proximity to corridors and service areas, openness of the floor plan, visibility, and the presence of technology that are divided into three categories (Table 7.1).

For measuring collaboration, Mattessich and Monsey's (2001) categories and Sawyer's (2017) indicators of collaboration have been selected. The choice to use the scales from these authors has been made based on the nature of the indicators to analyse and their suitability for measuring collaboration according to the model. The scale outcomes for measuring employee collaboration are listed in Table 7.2.

*Table 7.1* Collaborative environmental indicators.

| Collaborative Environment Satisfaction Items |
| --- |
| Teamwork related |
| Space layout related |
| Technology related |

Source: Authors' own, adapted from.

*Table 7.2* Employee collaboration outcomes.

| Outcomes | Mattesisch and Monsey (2001) | Sawyer (2017) |
| --- | --- | --- |
| Context | Environment | |
| Individuals | Membership characteristics | Being in control/ blending egos |
| Interaction processes | Communication | Communication |
| Structure | Process and structure | Equal participation |
| Support | Resources | |
| Tasks | | Complete concentration/ synergy |
| Teams | | Frequent interactions |

Source: Authors' own, adapted from Mattesisch and Monsey (2001) and Sawyer (2017).

### Hypotheses Questions

There are three main hypotheses questions, each of the hypotheses describing the relationship between the indicators for physical working environment and collaboration:

- H1: Does the space layout have a positive relationship with collaboration?
- H2: Does teamwork have a positive relationship with collaboration?
- H3. Is technology positively related to collaboration?

### Empirical Analysis

It has been decided to use the two-stage method (Wetzels et al., 2009; Ringle et al., 2012) for the empirical analysis of data. Therefore, first, the model assessment is evaluated through the exact test of goodness of fit and both reliability and validity of the measuring instrument are checked. After this, the structural model is assessed. The statistical analysis has been done through PLS-SEM in SmartPLS, a variance-based structural equation modelling approach as the main technique used to test the hypotheses. The main reason for using PLS-SEM is due to the characteristics of the composite construct included in the model. Both theoretical (Ringle et al., 2017) and empirical evidence (Ringle et al., 2017) support the use of PLS-SEM for models based on composites. For labelling the variables, both the physical working environment and collaboration have been defined as high-order composites measured in mode A, both at indicator and dimension level (Figure 7.1).

The measurement model is evaluated through the model assessment fit in PLS (Henseler et al., 2016). As Schubert et al. (2020) explain, for calculating the fit, the bootstrapping test has been used with P95 and P99 quantiles as critical values. After having obtained the results for the saturated model, the parameter scores for evaluating the model's reliability and validity have been calculated following the criteria for composites estimated in mode A: indicator reliability, internal consistency, convergent validity, and discriminant validity. Once the measuring model has been evaluated, the structural model has been next analysed. The structural model tests for the significance of the relationships between variables or the built hypotheses, and the model's predictivity over the endogenous variable's behaviour. For the analysis of the structural model, the coefficient of determination $R^2$ and path coefficients have been tested. In the same way, a power test has been done to calculate the effect size ($f^2$). The $f^2$ indicates the change in $R^2$ when a variable has been eliminated. In addition, the Bootstrap method has been used to assess the precision and the stability of the obtained estimators (Chin & Newsted, 1999) by analysing the significance of the direct effects. Finally, the blindfolding technique or Stone Geisser's test has been done to assess the predictive relevance of the path model (Hair et al., 2017).

## Results

As the results for the saturated model indicate, the model fits the collected data (Schubert et al., 2020). According to the results obtained for assessing reliability, the results in Table 7.3 show that most of the indicators meet the established values or the criteria for reliability (Carmines & Zeller, 1979). However, the indicators Processes1, Processes2, Support1, Teams0, and Teams1 have been eliminated from the analysis due to high correlation values.

Regarding composite reliability, all four composites show values higher than 0.6 (Barclay et al., 1995). About the results obtained for

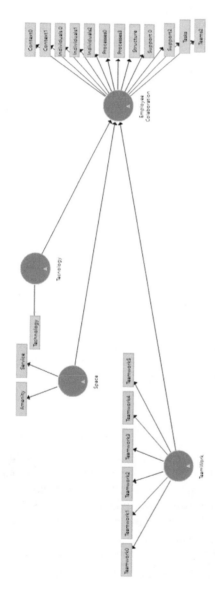

*Figure 7.1* Empirical model.
Source: Authors' own.

*Table 7.3* Results of reliability and validity analysis.

| Construct/Dimension/Indicator | Loading | Weight | CR | AVE |
|---|---|---|---|---|
| **Physical working environment (second-order composite in mode A at indicator level and dimension level)** | | | | |
| **Teamwork (Composite in mode A)** | | | 0.894 | 0.584 |
| Teamwork0 | $0.762^{***}$ | $0.188^{***}$ | | |
| Teamwork1 | $0.780^{***}$ | $0.225^{***}$ | | |
| Teamwork2 | $0.765^{***}$ | $0.218^{***}$ | | |
| Teamwork3 | $0.776^{***}$ | $0.228^{***}$ | | |
| Teamwork4 | $0.712^{***}$ | $0.195^{***}$ | | |
| Teamwork5 | $0.787^{***}$ | $0.253^{***}$ | | |
| **Space** | | | 0.857 | 0.749 |
| Amenity | $0.884^{***}$ | $0.614^{**}$ | | |
| Service | $0.847^{***}$ | $0.540^{**}$ | | |
| **Technology** | | | 1.000 | 1.000 |
| Technology | $1.000^{***}$ | $1.000^{***}$ | | |
| **Employee collaboration (composite in mode A)** | | | 0.928 | 0.520 |
| Context0 | $0.681^{***}$ | $0.112^{***}$ | | |
| Context1 | $0.766^{***}$ | $0.114^{***}$ | | |
| Individuals0 | $0.699^{***}$ | $0.077^{***}$ | | |
| Individuals1 | $0.820^{***}$ | $0.136^{***}$ | | |
| Individuals2 | $0.791^{***}$ | $0.136^{***}$ | | |
| Processes0 | $0.736^{***}$ | $0.113^{***}$ | | |
| Processes1 | Eliminated | | | |
| Processes2 | Eliminated | | | |
| Processes3 | $0.610^{***}$ | $0.146^{***}$ | | |
| Structure | $0.769^{***}$ | $0.127^{***}$ | | |
| Support0 | $0.747^{***}$ | $0.113^{***}$ | | |
| Support1 | Eliminated | | | |
| Support2 | $0.686^{***}$ | $0.110^{***}$ | | |
| Tasks | $0.739^{***}$ | $0.121^{***}$ | | |
| Teams0 | Eliminated | | | |
| Teams1 | Eliminated | | | |
| Teams2 | $0.562^{***}$ | $0.077^{***}$ | | |

Source: Authors' own.
*** significance at $p < 0.0001$ (two-tailed); ** significance at $p < 0.001$.

convergent validity, all values show an AVE (Average Variance Extracted) higher than the minimum of 0.5 (Hair et al., 2014). Regarding discriminant validity (Table 7.4) which has been measured by the HTMT (Heterotrait-Monotrait) criterion (Henseler et al., 2016), all indicators have values lower than the maximum of 0.85 (Hair et al., 2014). Therefore, the overall results support the model's validity as shown in Table 7.4.

*Table 7.4* Validity.

|  | EC | Space | Teamwork | Technology |
|---|---|---|---|---|
| Collaboration-EC | 0.721 | *0.415* | *0.850* | *0.281* |
| Space | 0.324 | 0.866 | *0.642* | *0.771* |
| Teamwork | 0.779 | 0.486 | 0.764 | *0.536* |
| Technology | 0.274 | 0.636 | 0.490 | 1.000 |

Source: Authors' own.

After the measurement, model has been assessed and reliability and validity of the model have been checked; the next step is to analyse the structural model. According to the results obtained for the structural model (Table 7.5), the model presents a $R^2$ value of 0.622 for collaboration, the dependent variable. The bootstrapping sample to check for the significance of the path coefficients shows that $T$-student values for the bootstrap coefficient are significant under the 1% significance level for the relationship between teamwork and collaboration (Table 7.5), so hypothesis 2 (H2) is accepted. However, the structural analysis has shown non-significant values for the relationship between space→collaboration ($T = 0.002$, $p = 0.499$) and technology→collaboration ($T = 1.170$, $p = 0.121$) and as a result, hypotheses H1 and H3 have been rejected. Regarding the effect size ($f^2$) there is a large effect size for teamwork→collaboration, a small effect size for technology→collaboration and no effect between space and collaboration thus also

*Table 7.5* Results for structural model.

| Hypotheses | β | T-Student | p value | CI Percentile | $f^2$ |
|---|---|---|---|---|---|
| H1. Space→ Collaboration | 0.000 | $0.002^{ns}$ | 0.499 | [−0.167; 0.225] | 0.000 |
| H2. Teamwork→ Collaboration | 0.848 | $12.522^{***}$ | 0.000 | [0.748; 0.960] | 1.347 |
| H3. Technology→ Collaboration | 0.141 | $1.170^{ns}$ | 0.121 | [−0.342; 0.040] | 0.029 |

Source: Authors' own.
$R^2$ (employee collaboration) = 0.622; $Q^2$ (employee collaboration) = 0.294
CI percentile, confidence interval
Hypothesized effects are assessed by applying a one-tailed test for distribution (CI: 95%)
$^{***}$ significance at $p < 0.001$, $^{ns}$ no significant.

corroborating teamwork as the most effective composite in relation to collaboration.

In addition, the results obtained for the Stone Geisser's test show a higher value than 0; therefore, it is assumed that the model has predictive ability.

## Conclusions

Regarding the outcomes selected for measuring the physical working environment and in relation to collaboration and teamwork, the results confirm there is a positive relationship between teamwork and collaboration. Therefore, hypothesis H2 is accepted. As the Bootstrap coefficient for the relationship between space and technology with collaboration has given non-significant values, hypotheses H1 and H3 have been rejected. It is possible to suggest that in relation to enhancing collaboration, the outcome with the best results for the physical working environment is teamwork. Although Hua (2010) considered spatial outcomes to mark the layouts that best influence collaboration and identified attributes that best describe collaborative environments, the most important spatial features are considerably those in relation to the variable teamwork as theory suggests (Salas et al., 2017). According to Hua (2010), the presence of conference and meeting rooms, open areas, and work groups intended for teamwork are the most important features of collaborative spaces in terms of enhancing their positive relationship to increase collaboration. Regarding the Mondragon Team Academy lab, the space is also structured into collaborative spatial features including shared desks and furniture and wireless technology available in the whole building. In addition, a team best functions when there is implication from the participating members and from the organization and it is therefore essential, the commitment from all members and students in the LEINN studying programme and the Mondragon Team Academy. This way, to enhance collaboration, team performance, and encourage initiatives like MTA, it is utterly important to continue with the study of the physical working environment in relation to different outcomes and throughout different work and studying settings.

The current COVID-19 pandemic, for example, has redefined workplaces and work environments into rethinking the concept of open space, highlighting the necessity of providing free-movement areas with mobile furniture and social distancing, minimizing the options for interaction and collaboration. However, wireless technology and online platforms have enabled to direct work and studying programmes to a whole virtual sphere thus, also rethinking the concept of collaboration that is now sustained by virtual and online-sharing platforms. The MTA has also suffered some of the consequences brought by the pandemic, and the physical proximity of the studying and participating members has been transferred into a virtual closeness where collaboration has continued to exist through the virtual world. However, due to the openness of the space and the options, it gives for remodelling and refurbishment of the furniture, placement of desks and the necessary material and social distancing, this has allowed the creation of permanent teams that can continue with their studying process and teamworking without the need to take special or added measures. Therefore, although the importance of the physical work environment has exponentially grown in the last years, there is still much to contribute to the scientific and academic literature by also considering the current situation, and other threats globalization can bring in the future. It is an interesting and challenging field of investigation that can bring surplus benefits and results to not only coworking spaces and Team Academy labs but also to many organizations worldwide.

## Notes

1 Google Headquarter in Palo Alto (California) is characterized by its key features on design, office distribution, and recreational areas.
2 Mondragon Team Academy (MTA): founded as part of the LEINN University program for entrepreneurship that has been recognized as one of the most important TeamLabs and team coaching of the world.

## References

Andriessen, E. (2003). *Working with groupware. Understanding and evaluating collaboration technology.* Berlin, Heidelberg, New York: Springer.
Barclay, D., Higgins, C., & Thompson, R. (1995). The partial least squares (PLS) approach to causal modelling: Personal computer adoption and use as an illustration. *Technology Studies, 2*(2), 285–309.
Becker, F. (2004). *Offices at work: Uncommon workspace strategies that add value and improve performance.* San Francisco, CA: Jossey-Bass.
Bender, D. (2013). *Mobile Arbeitsplätze als kreative Räume: Coworking spaces, Cafés und andere urbane Arbeitsorte.* Bielefeld: Transcript Verlag.
Brennan, A., Chugh, J. S., & Kline, T. (2002). Traditional versus Open Office design: A longitudinal field study. *Environment and Behavior, 34*(3), 279–299.
Carmines, E. G., & Zeller, R. A. (1979). Reliability and validity assessment. In *Sage university paper series on quantitative applications in the social sciences* (pp.7–17). Thousand Oaks, CA: SAGE Publications.

Cepeda Carrión, G., & Roldán-Salgueiro, J. L. (2004). Aplicando la técnica PLS en la administración de empresas. Conocimiento y competitividad. *Comunicación presentada en XIV congreso nacional de ACEDE, Murcia*, 74–78.

Chin, W. W., & Newsted, P. R. (1999). Structural equation modelling analysis with small samples using partial least squares. *Statistical strategies for small sample research* (pp. 307–341). Thousand Oaks, CA: SAGE Publications.

Fornell, C., & Larcker, D. F. (1981). Evaluating structural equation models with unobservable variables and measurement error. *Journal of Marketing Research, 18*(1), 39–50.

Foucault, M. (1967) Of other spaces. Michel Foucault and Jay Miskowiec. *Diacritics, 16*(1), 22–27 (Spring, 1986).

Gandini, A. (2015). The rise of coworking spaces: A literature review. *Ephemeral Journal, 15*(1), 193–205.

Gianna, S. D. (2014). La reproducción como categoría ontológica: Reflexiones desde la obra tardía de G. Lukács. *Rebela, 4*(1), 122. Retrieved November 15, 2016.

Hair, J.F., Hult, G.T.M., Ringle, C.M., & Sarstedt, M. (2017). *A primer on partial least squares structural equation modelling (PLS-SEM)*. Thousand Oaks, CA-London-New Delhi-Singapore: Sage Publications.

Hair, J. F., Sarstedt, M., & Kuppelwieser, V. (2014). Partial least squares structural equation modelling (PLS-SEM): An emerging tool for business research. *European Business Review, 26*(2), 106–121.

Heerwagen, J. H., Kampschroer, K., Powell, K. M., & Loftness, V. (2004). Collaborative knowledge work environments. *Building Research and Innovation, 23*(6), 510–528.

Hennemann, E. A., Lee, J. L., & Cohen, J. (1995). Collaboration a concept analysis. *Journal of Advanced Nursing, 23*(1), 103–109.

Henseler, J., Hubona, G., & Ray, P. (2016). Using PLS math modelling in new technology research: Updated guidelines. *Industrial Management & Data Systems, 116*(1), 2–20.

Henseler, J., Ringle, C., & Sincoviks, R. (2009). The use of partial least squares path modelling in international marketing. *New Challenges to International Marketing, 20*, 277–319.

Hu, L.-t., & Bentler, P. M. (1999). Cutoff criteria for fit indexes in covariance structure analysis: Conventional criteria versus new alternatives. *Structural Equation Modelling, 6*(1), 1–55.

Hua, Y. (2010). A model of workplace environment satisfaction, collaboration experience, perceived collaboration effectiveness: A survey instrument. *International Journal of Facility Management, 1*(2), 1–21.

Hua, Y., Kraut, R., Loftness, V., & Powell, K. M. (2010). Workplace collaborative space layout typology and occupant perception of collaborative environment. *Environment and Planning B: Planning and Design, 37*(3), 429–448.

Kaiser, S., Ringlstetter, M., Eikhof, D., & Pina e Cunha, M. (Eds). *Creating Balance* (pp. 269–284). Berlin, Heidelberg: Springer.

Latham, G. P. (2007). *Foundations for organizational science. Work motivation: History, theory, research, and practice*. Thousand Oaks, CA: Sage Publications, Inc.

Lefebvre, H. (1905). *The production of space*. Oxford: Wiley (ed.).

Lyotard, J. F. (1984). *The postmodern condition: A report on knowledge* (Vol. 10 of Theory and history of literature). Minnesota: University of Minnesota Press.

Mattesisch, P. W., & Monsey, B. R. (2001). *Collaboration: What makes it work: A review of research literature on factors influencing successful collaboration*. St. Paul, MN: Amherst H. Wilder Foundation. First published in 1992 by Amherst H. Wilder Foundation, St. Paul, Minnesota.

Oldham, G. R., & Brass, D. J. (1979). Employee reactions to an Open-Plan Office: A naturally occurring quasi-experiment. *Administrative Science Quarterly, 6*(2), 267–284.

Ringle, C. M., Sarstedt, M., Mitchell, R., & Gudergan, S. P. (2017). Partial least squares structural equation modelling in HRM research. *The International Journal of Human Resource Management, 27*(1), 1617–1643.

Ringle, C. M., Sarstedt, M., & Straub, D. W. (2012). Editor's comments: A critical look at the use of PLS-SEM in MIS Quarterly. *MIS Quarterly, 36*(1), 3–14.

Salas, E., Rico, R., & Passmore, J. (2017). *The Wiley Blackwell handbook of the psychology of team working and collaborative processes*. Hoboken, NJ: John Wiley & Sons Ltd. First published in 2010 by John Wiley & Sons Ltd.

Sawyer, K. (2017). *Group genius: The creative power of collaboration*. New York: Basic Books.

Schrage, M. (1990). *Shared minds: The new technologies of collaboration*. New York: Random House.

Schubert, F., Rademaker, M. E., & Henseler, J. (2020). Estimating and assessing second-order constructs using PLS-PM: The case of composites of composites. *Journal of Industrial Management and Data System, 120*(12), 2211–2241.

Townsend, A. M., Demarie, S. M., & Hendrickson, A. R. (1998). Virtual teams: Technology and the workplace of the future. *Academy of Management Perspective, 12*(3), 17–29.

Vera, J. S. (2000). *Creative collaboration*. New York: Oxford University Press.

Wetzels, M., Odekerken-Schröder, G., & Van Oppen, C. (2009). Using PLS path modelling for assessing hierarchical construct models: Guidelines and empirical illustrations. *MIS Quarterly, 33*, 177–195.

# 8 Dimensions of Leadership: Team Academies as Systems

*Péter Tasi and Ann-Cathrin Scheider*

## Introduction

Leadership in team academies is a challenge for team coaches and students. The programme facilitates a self-driven approach of learning. Students are encouraged to act on and grow their personal initiative and self-efficacy working in teams, starting companies, and engaging in real business. Such a programme calls for leadership on many levels. However, the different expectations and needs of all parties involved do not leave room for easy solutions. This chapter aims to give new insights on leadership in team academies using a theoretical systemic approach.

For team coaches, students, and future programme leaders, the understanding of team academies as systems can help to further shape their personal approach to leadership and facilitation of leadership development.

## The Leadership Challenge and What Systems Have to Do with It

From our practice as team coaches, we have known that leadership is a central topic in team academies, and to be honest, we were surprised by how important it was. The Team Academy programme as an art of entrepreneurship education is designed to facilitate building entrepreneurial skills. Leadership is often treated merely as a side-effect. Also, in the EntreComp Model,[1] one of the most popular entrepreneurial skills-based models created by the European Union, leadership is also not mentioned as a specific skill (Bacigalupo et al., 2016). It seems that leadership is less of a skill, but more of an antecedent of entrepreneurial skills.

In management theory, we find numerous definitions which focus on one person who is in charge. In team academies though, we work with

DOI: 10.4324/9781003163121-8

shared and rotating leadership. The underlying belief is that for really innovative companies a large skillset is needed which cannot be found in only one leading person.

We have also experienced that the leadership of the programme itself poses numerous challenges. Falling into the trap of traditional leadership often leads to overregulation and bureaucracy within the programme. Therefore, leadership in team academies must be viewed in a different light.

When taking a bird's-eye perspective on team academies, we can identify different dimensions or layers. In this regard, we argue that each Team Academy can be seen as a system with a number of team companies forming sub-systems, together creating a social system to bring about a totally different model of studying.

Scharmer in his book *Theory U* proposes different layers of social systems: the mundo-level with global systemic action, the macro-level with institutional action, the meso-level with communicative action, and the micro-level with thinking action (Scharmer, 2015). Lending this view on social systems, we analyse the different dimensions with regard to leadership in team academies in the following sections. We focus on the macro-, meso-, and micro-levels of the system to find new insights on leadership on these levels.

For our purposes, we adapted the layers as follows:

- Macro-level: the Team Academy programme in a respective university
- Meso-level: the team companies in a given Team Academy, as well as the project groups within a team company
- Micro-level: the individual team entrepreneur

## Leading to Coach

The overall aim of the Team Academy is to enable self-driven entrepreneurship education for individuals and teams. Entrepreneurship requires flexibility, adaptability, and constant change which stands in strong contrast to the bureaucratic education systems the programmes are embedded in.

Coming from this background it is not surprising that on the macro-level, representing the programme itself, there often seems to be a struggle to find a balance between visionary and bureaucratic leadership. This tension leads to overregulation and rigidity on the one hand or laissez-faire on the other.

In view of this challenge, team coaches are required to adopt different roles within the dimensions of their particular Team Academy.

On the macro-level, the team coaches represent a leadership team. But how can we, as team coaches, effectively lead the programme to facilitate entrepreneurial learning?

Generally, entrepreneurship education aims at enabling students to effectively pursue entrepreneurial opportunity. According to Venkataraman, entrepreneurial opportunity is determined by taking action with high uncertainty, ambiguity, and risk (Venkataraman, 1997).

Here we want to make a link to complex adaptive systems, a concept first used in computing. Complex adaptive systems change and reorganize their parts to adapt themselves to problems posed by their surroundings. These systems are directed at a moving aim, which makes it difficult to control or lead them (Holland, 1992). We believe a lot can be gained from looking at team academies as complex adaptive systems. This bird's-eye view gives us the opportunity to see what kind of leadership is really needed for the Team Academy to bring about self-efficacy and initiative with all parties involved.

Complex adaptive systems aim to constantly evolve with people in such a system interacting with each other on their way of going towards a shared vision. Leadership can therefore not be attributed to a single person influencing others. Instead, it is enacted through complex interactions within the system and is seen as emerging (Lichtenstein, 2006). With hierarchy playing no or a subordinate role, shared interests or goals bring together different people and stand in the centre of all action and interaction.

With some insight on complex adaptive systems and integration of the complexity leadership theory, we argue that leadership on the macro-level comes down to initiating processes. Case studies on complex systems leadership in emergent community projects showed that the leaders of these systems took an active role in initiating the project and therefore were trusted as people of integrity who were believed to strive to achieve the best for the shared interest. The project initiators had an informal authority to start processes as the communities developed (Onyx & Leonard, 2010).

In team academies, there is a crucial emphasis on dialogue in teams. We see dialogue as a tool of creating shared understanding, and also thinking together. Through dialogue, we can tap into a field of opportunities, ideas, and understandings which would otherwise be invisible and inaccessible (Isaac, 1999). Viewing a Team Academy as a complex system offers the chance to see that these interactions represent the foundation of approaching leadership. In that regard, dialogue is not merely a way of understanding each other and creating together, but a way of leading the system.

Lichtenstein et al. also propose three pillars for leadership in complex adaptive systems: collective identity, tension, and leadership events. All of these pillars constitute focused interaction, which can be initiated through dialogue. In this light, we want to highlight the concept of the leading thoughts from the Finnish Tiimiakatemia.[2] In this concept, it is proposed to initiate dialogue on values, vision and mission to find a shared understanding for different topics that are relevant to the whole system. Values define how the team functions, whether and how the team keeps on the right track. Vision covers the common goal, the direction where the team goes. Mission is the core element of a team's existence (Toivanen, 2012). By doing this, all parties involved together shape the collective identity of the Team Academy. The creation of which must be conceived as a process that is repeatedly negotiated through activation of the relationships that link the people and groups in a system (Melucci, 1995).

We argue that the creation of a collective identity is a key process of leadership on the macro-level. As leaders of the programme, we are the ones to initiate such a process, without falling into the trap of stepping into a traditional leadership role.

Team coaches work very closely with the team entrepreneurs. The relationship is distinctly different from other professor-student relationships. If we follow the argument of community leadership, we can assume that the trust towards the initiating team coaches is rather high. In this case, all initiatives coming from the team coaches have a slightly higher priority than those coming from other parts of the system. This powerful position within the system can and, we argue, should be used for the best interest of all.

## One for All and All for One

At team company level leadership plays a significant role from at least two aspects. One of them is the legal aspect which is mostly determined by the legal form of the team company. In Germany, the cooperative needs a board of directors consisting of three persons, which is supported by a supervisory board. Together they have the full legal responsibility for all the cooperative's actions. It is obvious that the existing difference within tasks and responsibilities influences differences between team members, but as team companies are usually founded as cooperatives, legally all founders and members are equal. To avoid the undesirable consolidation of hierarchy there is a rotation in the legal leadership positions over the duration of the Team Academy programme. This systematic change offers the possibility for each team entrepreneur to try themselves in a leadership position and encourages adaptability. Based on team coaches' experiences, teams need some time to find their way of accessing the leadership topic in their own team companies. Especially in the starting phase, we can identify at least three types of behaviour:

- Team entrepreneurs with natural leadership qualities, who also take on leadership roles immediately.
- Team entrepreneurs with leadership skills who remain in the background at first. Usually, to get to know the team more to gain confidence or they consciously decide to leave the leadership roles for others who have, in their eyes, more learning need and potential.
- Students with no identified leadership qualities. Usually, they stay out of leadership positions as their goal is first to gain experience and learn what leadership means.

This orientation phase can be seen as the first phase of emergent leadership, another form of complexity leadership. This type of leadership describes a leadership phenomenon of a team leader arising informally (Hoch & Dulebohn, 2017). In the orientation phase, the informal leaders are identified by the group and a dynamic of teamwork is started. Authority, is therefore, given by the group and significant influence of the informal leaders is accepted (Schneider & Goktepe, 1983). Csillag et al. (2019) indicate that owners of small firms have a key role in establishing workplace conditions which in turn influence learning possibilities in the firm. Through emergent rotating leadership, all team members share the responsibility in shaping their workplace conditions towards reaching their common learning goal: experiencing entrepreneurship and entrepreneurial leadership.

After the orientation phase, some of the informal leaders may continue to influence the development of the team and team company (Smart, 2005). At the same time, it can be seen that this influence becomes smaller as the team progresses in the phases of team development (Pescosolido, 2001). In team companies, we see that the influence of informal leaders shrinks, as the team progresses from emergent leadership to rotating entrepreneurial leadership.

If we assume that teams start with emergent leadership and then move into entrepreneurial leadership through role formulation and attribution, it is very important to focus on which competencies are necessary for this type of leadership. Gupta et al. created one of the early definitions, focusing on activities rather than roles. In the focus of their definition of entrepreneurial leadership lies the creation of visionary scenarios. They argue that the vision motivates supporters to commit to the discovery of opportunities for the strategic creation of value (Gupta et al., 2004).

As the topic of entrepreneurial leadership is relatively young, researchers are still trying to find out more about what really constitutes entrepreneurial leadership, and there exist numerous definitions (Leitch & Volery, 2016). To find out what is most important to team entrepreneurs when it comes to entrepreneurial leadership, we gathered insights from a small sample of 20 students. On a 6-point scale ranging from 1 = not important for leadership to 6 = most important for leadership, we asked the students which of the entrepreneurial skills in the EntreComp model (Bacigalupo et al., 2016) they consider most important for entrepreneurial leadership. Our students rated all entrepreneurial skills to be higher than 4 = quite important, very important, or most important. From this, we concluded that the proposed entrepreneurial skills equal the students' desired leadership qualities.

To find out more, we asked another sample which characteristics are expected from leaders in team companies. This time we wanted the students to come up with their own expectations. Within individual coaching sessions with 40 members from four different team companies' sessions at the Team Academy in Bremerhaven, we used the method of the Leadership Pizza[3] to investigate this question. The method offers a visual and intuitive way of dealing with expectations towards leaders and leadership. Each team member got a hypothetical pizza on which they could place their expectations. In our round of coaching sessions, all team members followed the course of the method and shared eight characteristics (as eight slices of a pizza) of a leader, what they really expect while being led in a team. From these coaching interviews, we collected 105 different types of characteristics after filtering out similar word usage. In the next step, the frequency of mention of each trait with the number of respondents was calculated.

In the following figure, we can see what proportion of the respondents from the four teams named these most frequently mentioned characteristics overall.

Interestingly, especially the characteristics referring to smaller businesses, which can be found in the literature, such as accountability, networking skills, balancing global and local perspectives (Chandler et al., 2019) did not all emerge in the coaching interviews. However, the students mentioned empathy as the most important skill of leadership in entrepreneurial teams.

To understand how the mentioned characteristics correspond to the competencies defined in the EntreComp model of the EU, we tried to match the leadership expectations to the entrepreneurial competencies of the model (Bacigalupo et al., 2016). Table 8.1 summarizes the relationships that were identified.

Allocating the leadership expectations of the team entrepreneurs to the entrepreneurial competencies of the EntreComp, we found that the students did not mention any expectation that could be matched to creativity, mobilizing resources, coping with uncertainty, risk and ambiguity as well as learning through experience. It is interesting that in a learning-by-doing based education model, responding team entrepreneurs did not mention the competence itself, and did not mention competence related to risk-taking either, although one of the features of the training is that making mistakes is not a problem or even an opportunity.

*Table 8.1* Comparing competences and expected characteristics (based on Bacigalupo et al., 2016). Data from interviews with students of the Bachelor "Entrepreneurship, Innovation, Leadership" at Bremerhaven University of Applied Sciences (2021).

| Competences at EntreComp Model | Expected Characteristics of a Leader at TA |
| --- | --- |
| Spotting opportunities | Decisiveness |
| Creativity | |
| Vision | Vision |
| Valuing ideas | Appreciation |
| Ethical and sustainable thinking | Authenticity |
| | Responsibility |
| Self-awareness and self-efficacy | Self-confidence |
| Motivation and perseverance | Motivation |
| Mobilizing resources | |
| Financial and economic literacy | Expert |
| Mobilizing others | Inspiration/curiosity |
| | Delegation |
| Taking the initiative | Passion |
| Planning and management | Have an overview |
| Coping with uncertainty, ambiguity, and risk | |
| Working with others | Team player |
| | Empathy |
| | Friendship/good relationship |
| | Communication |
| Learning through experience | |

Source: Authors' own.

In this current phase, we can conclude that there are similarities and differences between the responses of the participants in the Team Academy programme and the leadership characteristics defined in the literature. These differences, which are significant in some respects, raise the possibility and need for further research to reveal the reasons for the differences and to examine the impact of these differences on the training itself and the development of the leadership skills of the participants in teams and also as individuals.

## But First: Self-leadership

At micro-level individual team members, the so-called team entrepreneurs are responsible for taking charge of their own learning process. This learning process can be understood only within the team, also in connection with the taken and shared responsibility for each other. Following the assumption that individual learning improves the performance of the whole team and that leadership can facilitate and guide this learning, learning and leadership come together at each level (Knipfer et al., 2018).

In the picture of the complex adaptive system, it is crucial for team entrepreneurs being able to adapt to a fast-changing environment in order to spot and exploit entrepreneurial opportunities. Unlike other programmes, there are no clear rules and guidelines on how to study team entrepreneurship. In order to be able to finish the course, the student has to work on their capacity of self-leadership. This involves the self-motivation and self-direction needed to obtain desired results (Manz, 1992). The self-influence excerpted here subsumes the behaviour-focused strategies of self-regulation, self-control, and self-management (Houghton & Neck, 2002). We often see that it is challenging for the teams that there is no consequence if someone does not perform. Expectations are highly subjective (Figure 8.1) and even if the team sets their expectations, it is up to each team entrepreneur if they want to live up to those expectations. Therefore, being able to turn intrinsic motivation into action plays a crucial role. Lovelace et al. (2007) argue that in order to facilitate shared leadership and reduce demands towards a leader, it is helpful to improve the self-leadership capacity of the team.

Following the steps of "do-think-learn progress" within the process of the experimenting, we highlight three important elements of improving the self-leadership of individual team entrepreneurs:

- Goal-setting: It helps to define where team entrepreneurs want to go and what they want to exactly achieve. The goals are mostly for

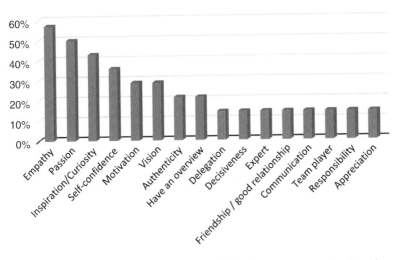

*Figure 8.1* Expected characteristics of a leader in team companies (based on SessionLab, 2020).

Source: Authors' own.

the period spent at the Team Academy but can also be longer term. Usually, goals are set following the SMART[4] principle.

- Self-reflection: In written form or live at team trainings (group meetings), its role is to give the possibility for the team entrepreneur to think seriously over behaviour, actions, learning, work, experiences and after those to find out what is going well and what could be still improved.
- Feedback: In this process element, the team entrepreneur compares inputs with outputs of activities as well as the self-reflection with the feedback from others and attempts to explore causal relationships.

Throughout the programme, team entrepreneurs learn more and more how to lead and manage themselves in an effective and healthy way. Prussia et al. (1998) identified self-efficacy as a mediating factor between self-leadership and performance outcome. In our understanding, the increase of self-efficacy is in the very centre of the intended outcomes of Team Academy programmes. Concluding, the programme itself can and should lead to improved self-leadership. By bringing business ideas to customers, making cold calls, and earning money in the team, the team entrepreneurs are challenged to improve on their self-leadership as a necessity to their success both as a team and individually. Taking this into account, we believe that self-leadership should be stressed especially in the beginning of the programme to get the team entrepreneurs started. The team coaches can support their students by addressing the topic in their coaching sessions as well as, in the complexity leadership fashion, initiating events that foster the self-leadership skills.

Progressing through the programme, the team entrepreneurs will then increase their self-leadership capacity by actively engaging in their team companies and focusing on performance outcomes.

## Conclusion

Team Academy programmes are aimed at enabling a new form of self-driven learning and learning in teams. The learning platform is a team company operating as a real business. The challenges and learning opportunities are plentiful just as the characters of the individual team entrepreneurs, team coaches and stakeholders that make up the Team Academy as a social (eco-) system. The complexity inherent led us to looking at team academies through the lens of complex adaptive systems. To keep complex systems adaptive, it is necessary to work together within the system. Leadership in these systems varies through the dimensions of the system. Through our analysis, we were able to understand the team academies from a bird's-eye perspective and see the most important responsibilities and tasks of the actors in another light.

At macro-level, team coaches should aim to lead by initiating processes, creating, and offering flexible frameworks for the community of Team Academy as a whole, for team companies as well as teams, and for the entrepreneurial development of individual team entrepreneurs.

At meso-level, team entrepreneurs in a team discover and experience leadership as a fundamental element of entrepreneurial behaviour. Based on common learnings gained within the team, they should reflect on the emergent quality of leadership in their team companies. The experience gained by acting as a leader and being led within the Team Academy contributes to the development of self-efficacy and success of the team on the one hand, and lays the foundation for team entrepreneurs to be better able to organize themselves as a team on the other.

At micro-level, individual team entrepreneurs should learn and improve their self-leadership competence especially at the beginning of the programme. This competence is actively used in the later stages of their learning process to organize themselves, achieve their goals, and learn effectively.

We found that adopting a systemic view offers one way of dealing with the complexity of the Team Academy programme. We believe that the systemic view proposed in this article can serve as a starting point for dialogue among programme leaders, team coaches, and team entrepreneurs, within team academies. But also between team academies and in other entrepreneurship education programmes where participants learn and explore in teams.

## Notes

1 EntreComp Model was developed by the European Union and defines entrepreneurship as a competence in three different areas/levels, such as "Ideas and opportunities", "Resources", and "Into action". More about this at: https://ec.europa.eu/jrc/en/publication/eur-scientific-and-technical-research-reports/entrecomp-entrepreneurship-competence-framework
2 Team Academy (or Tiimiakatemia in Finnish) was originally developed by Johannes Partanen in Jyväskylä, Finland in 1993. As a unique entrepreneurial team learning and learning-by-doing based education model, it now shapes a worldwide network. More about the original Tiimiakatemia at: https://www.tiimiakatemia.fi/en
3 Detailed information, description of the method, and its application can be found at https://www.sessionlab.com/methods/leadership-pizza.
4 SMART stands for specific, measurable, achievable, realistic, timely. Please note that there are other explanations as well.

## References

Bacigalupo, M., Kampylis, P., Punie, Y., & Van Den Brande, L. (2016) EntreComp: The Entrepreneurship Competence Framework. Luxembourg: Publications Office of the European Union. Retrieved February 10, 2021, from https://ec.europa.eu/jrc/en/publication/eur-scientific-and-technical-research-reports/entrecomp-entrepreneurship-competence-framework

Chandler, N., Mosolygó-Kiss, Á., & Heidrich, B. (2019) Ensuring sustainable growth: The transference of responsible leadership characteristics during family business succession. IECER conference, October, 16–18, 2019, Utrecht, conference paper. Retrieved February 20, 2021, from https://www.researchgate.net/publication/336837416_Ensuring_sustainable_growth_the_transference_of_responsible_leadership_characteristics_during_family_business_succession

Csillag, S., Csizmadia, P., Hidegh, A. L., & Szászvári, K. Á. (2019). What makes small beautiful? Learning and development in small firms. *Human Resource Development International*, *22*(5), 453–476. doi:10.1080/13678868.2019.1641351.

## 124   *Péter Tasi and Ann-Cathrin Scheider*

Gupta, V., McMillan, I., & Surie, G. (2004) Entrepreneurial leadership: Developing and measuring a crosscultural construct. *Journal of Business Venturing 19*(2), 241–260. doi:10.1016/S0883-9026(03)00040-5.

Hoch, J., & Dulebohn, J. (2017). Team personality composition, emergent leadership and shared leadership in virtual teams: A theoretical framework. *Human Resource Management Review, 27,* 678–693. doi:10.1016/j.hrmr.2016.12.012.

Houghton, J., & Neck, C. (2002). The revised self-leadership questionnaire: Testing a hierarchical factor structure for self-leadership. *Journal of Managerial Psychology, 17*(8), 642–691. doi:10.1108/02683940210450484.

Holland, J. (1992). Complex adaptive systems. *Daedalus, 121*(1), 17–30. A New Era in Computation. https://www.jstor.org/stable/20025416

Isaac, W. (1999). *Dialogue: The art of thinking together.* New York: Double Day.

Knipfer, K., Schreiner, E., Schmid, E., & Peus, C. (2018). The performance of pre-founding entrepreneurial teams: The importance of learning and leadership. *Applied Psychology, 67*(3), 401–427. doi:10.1111/apps.12126.

Leitch, C. M., & Volery, T. (2016). Entrepreneurial leadership: Insights and directions. *International Small Business Journal, 35*(2), 147–156. doi:10.1177/0266242616681397.

Lichtenstein, B., Uhl-Bien, M., Marion, R., Seers, A., & Orton, J. D. (2006). *Complexity leadership theory: An interactive perspective on leading in complex adaptive systems.* Lincoln: Management Department Faculty Publications, University of Nebraska.

Lovelace, K., Manz, C., & Alves, J. (2007). Work stress and leadership development: The role of self-leadership, shared leadership, physical fitness and flow in managing demands and increasing job control. *Human Resource Management Review, 17*(2007), 374–387. doi:10.1016/j.hrmr.2007.08.001.

Manz, C. (1992). *Mastering self-leadership: Empowering yourself for personal excellence.* Englewood Cliffs, NJ: Prentice-Hall.

Melucci, A. (1995). The process of collective identity. *Social movements and culture: Social movements: Protest & contention.* London: Routledge.

Onyx, J., & Leonard, R. J. (2010). Complex systems leadership in emergent community projects. *Community Development Journal, 46*(4), 493–510. doi:10.1093/cdj/bsq041.

Partanen, J. (2012). *The Team Coach's Best Tools,* Partus Tiimiakatemia. Jyvaskylä: Kopijyva Oy.

Pescosolido, A. T. (2001). Informal leaders and the development of group efficacy. *Small Group Research, 32*(1), 74–93. doi:10.1177/104649640103200104.

Prussia, G., Anderson, J., & Manz, C. (1998). Self-leadership and performance outcomes: The mediating influence of self-efficacy. *Journal of Organizational Behavior, 19,* 523–538. 10.1002/(SICI)1099-1379(199809)19:5<523::AID-JOB860>3.0.CO;2-I

Scharmer, C. O. (2015). *Theorie U. Von der Zukunft her führen: Presencing als soziale Technik [Öffnung des Denkens, Öffnung des Fühlens, Öffnung des Willens],* Vol. 4. Aufl. Heidelberg: Carl Auer.

Schneider, C. E., & Goktepe, J. R. (1983). Issues in emergent leadership: The contingency model of leadership, leader sex, leader behavior. In H. H. Blumberg, A. P. Hare, V. Kent, & M. F. Davies (Eds), *Small groups and social interaction* (Vol. 1, pp. 413–421). Chichester, UK: John Wiley.

SessionLab (2020). Leadership pizza method. Retrieved November 14, 2020, from https://www.sessionlab.com/methods/leadership-pizza

Smart, M. (2005). The role of informal leaders in organizations: The hidden organizational asset, PhD dissertation. Idaho: University of Idaho.

Toivanen, H. (2012). *Friend leadership: A visual inspiration book*. Vaasa: Oy Fram Ab.

Venkataraman, S. (1997). The distinctive domain of entrepreneurship research: An editor's perspective. In J. et Katz & R. Brockhaus (Eds), *Advances in entrepreneurship, firm emergence, and growth* (Vol. 3, pp. 119–138). Greenwich, CT: JAI Press.

# 9 Part II: The Phenomenon of "I as Leader" in the Team Academy Model: Characteristics and Attributes

*Karolina Ozadowicz*

## Introduction

Team Academy programmes offer a particular environment where *leading* can be practised. The key element of that environment is self-managed entrepreneurial teams supported by a Team Coach. Team Academy programmes are student-led with learners deciding for themselves what direction and shape their activities will take. The culture of Team Academy programmes is such that they act as a cradle in which leaders grow and develop. This culture is based on strong personal relationships and acts as a base from where learners can experiment with their understanding of self and others.

To achieve clarity of the discussion, first, this chapter will provide an overview of the concept of a leader in general terms. I then investigate it more closely giving the priority to exploring the role of a leader in the context of Team Academy programmes.

The notion of leader will be discussed using examples and reflections gathered during the author's involvement with one of the Team Academy-based programmes placed in the University of the West of England, Bristol, called *Team Entrepreneurship.*

This article is based on the analyses of the author's reflective journal entries since joining Team Entrepreneurship in 2015.

## Leaders in the Team Academy Model

There are numerous definitions of who a leader is (Rus et al., 2010). Perhaps the best-known approach uniting various perspectives is proposed by Goleman et al. (2012) who point most effective leaders are alike in one crucial way, i.e. having a high ability to be aware of, control, and express emotions, and to handle interpersonal relationships judiciously and empathetically. Goleman calls this ability

DOI: 10.4324/9781003163121-9

emotional intelligence. In the particular context of Team Academy, instead of focusing purely on a leader as a person, it might be more appropriate to include conceptualization where leadership is a collective process shaped in the interaction between all team members. This is in line with Carsten et al. (2010) who note anyone can be a source of leadership but the extent to which one is that source will vary depending on individual schemas with the participation ranging from passive and deferent to engaged and proactive (Carsten & Uhl-Bien, 2013).

This conceptualization might bring confusion and even resistance due to the popularity of so-called the *Great Man* theory of leadership (Organ, 1996). These theories promoted over many years became the *common knowledge* and the *approved* way the general public interprets and understands the phenomenon of a leader. These focused on studying not leadership as a dynamic process but almost exclusively explored the concept of a leader as an individual. The main message of the *Great Man* theory of leadership is that leaders are born, not made, are somehow *special,* often in a position of power, ultimately responsible for the success or failure of their organizations or teams and tasked with *showing the way.* The theories focused on exploring the *Great Man* can be divided into two main strands: traits and styles.

Research on traits studied and categorizes leaders depending on their personality traits. These approaches are often built on the so-called *Big Five* model (De Raad, 2000) describing an individual's personality using measures of five characteristics: conscientiousness, agreeableness, emotional stability, extraversion, and openness to experience (Judge & Bono, 2000). In a way, each of these traits can be described as a quality each individual possesses to different degrees. In the Team Entrepreneurship programme, reflection is used to support students in building awareness around these qualities. The team members are encouraged to explore these through self-observation either in their written assignments or dialogue sessions at the Training Sessions.

The research on styles examines leaders by examining how leaders act rather than their personalities. In the Team Academy programmes, interactions between students occur through the use of dialogue (Isaacs, 1999) and circle processes (Pranis, 2015). Use of this *inclusive* team's approaches means any attempt of leading with the autocratic and/or authoritative style is rejected with such individuals often criticized and even marginalized by the others. At Team Entrepreneurship (the Team Academy programme based in Bristol) within the remaining leader's styles (i.e. laissez-faire, pacesetting, democratic, coaching, affiliative), particular attention is given to promoting the coaching style of leading. Until 2020, students (referred to in Bristol as Team Entrepreneurs (TEs)) would have taken part in formal coaching training aimed at equipping them with the skill of coaching. Recently, formal coaching training has been removed with TEs developing competencies in coaching through being introduced to coaching models and practising these in their Training Sessions encouraged to use coaching approaches in discussions and interaction with other team members. Students often comment on the skill of asking questions (asking open-ended questions is one of the main competencies of coaching) and that use of curiosity and the attitude of being open-minded instead of claiming they know all of the right answers creates a sense of task ownership, feeling of fairness and equality in the team, altogether enhancing their experience on the programme.

One of the academics known for his contribution to the development of research on leadership styles is Bernard Bass and in particular, his Full Range Leadership Model (1985). The review of Bass's work was undertaken by, among others, Cummings et al. (2018), who categorized leadership styles into two main groups. The first category of leadership styles focuses on human relationships and the second one on task completion.

Within relationally focused leadership three styles of leading were named: transformational, resonant, authentic. Transformational leadership is described as a style which maximizes the potential of individuals through the encouragement of innovation, creativity and intellectual stimulation (Bass & Avolio, 1994). In the context of entrepreneurial teams based on the Team Academy principles, this style is witnessed most often when very ambitious learners act as an example to others and inspire them to take action. Such leaders will share their own stories of how dedication, discipline, commitment and passion helped them achieve success. Their sharings, frequently in Training Sessions, is what motivates others. Most often the team members don't realize they lead by being an example to each other and how profound an impact their stories have on others in the team. As one student shared:

> *When you are part of the programme is like you are in the bubble – you are unable to see the effects the programme has on you and there is nothing else to compare it with. It's only when you are out and the programme ends you see how much you were given and how much you miss it.* (Ozadowicz, 2018)[1]

Resonant leadership focuses on understanding the needs of individuals (Boyatzis et al., 2005; Goleman et al., 2002). This is by far the most common style in the Team Entrepreneurship programme in Bristol. The majority of the students demonstrate the ability to relate to their colleagues on the team, understanding their needs and difficulties and most often, being extremely accommodating. The results of the use of this style are not always positive. On the contrary, often, such a style of contribution to the leadership processes turns into underperformance and avoidance of responsibility. It can be observed, especially, early on in the process of team formation (L1), TEs don't want to offend each other and somehow feel that as they are peers they don't have *the right* to hold each other to account or simply not want to appear to think they are at a higher i.e. *better* level or *above the others.*

Avolio and Gardner (2005) notice the authentic leadership style frequently develops as a response to hindered in a transformational leadership risk of manipulation. This particular style of leading emphasizes leader transparency, and congruence in actions and beliefs (Avolio & Gardner, 2005). Students in Bristol seem to appreciate this style. Some team entrepreneurs speak of *radical transparency* often choosing honesty as one of their team's main values. To support the culture of openness and transparency, most teams will run regular feedback sessions (by one team named *Storming* Sessions). Using 360 Feedback team would meet regularly to discuss their behaviour and how it impacts their team performance. Although at times, uncomfortable, students often share how much they look forward to these sessions and how they *clear the air* and support them with focusing their energies more effectively on this which moves their teams forward. George (2016), a renowned advocate of authenticity, described authentic leaders as individuals who clearly understand who they are, and thus the impact they have on other people. Often, participants of the Team Academy Programmes comment on how the programme helps them to develop the curiosity of self and deep desire to increase their level of self-awareness which in turn supports them in leading authentically and with honesty. After all, *"leadership comes with the mastery of the self, and so developing leadership is a process of developing the self"* (Kouzes & Posner, 2008, p. 298). The ability of team members to be honest and open with each other increases over time. Usually, L1 students remain more polite rather than honest with each other. Next to supporting the team with the formation of the relationship and building trust, one of the main roles of the Team Coach in L1 is to bring up pretentiousness to the surfaces and make it visible. This might be as simple as asking team members: *What is that you are not saying each other?* or *When you say "we" didn't to it, who is the "we"? Who are you really talking to? Would you be ready to repeat this statement using the names of the individuals?*

Within the task-focused leadership style, the following are included: transactional leadership, in which leaders make a transaction with followers by providing rewards in exchange for tasks completion (Bass & Avolio, 1994), dissonant leadership styles, whereby leaders employ commanding and pace-setting behaviours to achieve results (Goleman et al., 2002), and instrumental leadership that focuses on bridging motivational vision with strategic and task-mediated accomplishment (Avolio, 1999). Task-focused leadership styles (passive or dissonant) are generally associated with adverse outcomes. These styles can prevail when students are *made* to take part in the activities offered by the programme and which they find little interest in. When such mismatch of interests occurs, the passive and dissonant styles are often emerging. Interestingly, students are often aware of this and openly admit their contribution to such projects is minimal and only extended to the minimum standards required of them. As a result, students will contribute poorly to the leadership processes and ultimately this will have an impact on the quality of the outcome. These unsuccessful engagements in the leadership process, however frustrating for the other team members and perhaps even the Team Coach, often strengthens the leadership processes in the long term. The team members are encouraged to learn from their unsuccessful engagement and on the future tasks implement changes so that the same mistakes are not made. This might include things like choosing entrepreneurial activities the whole team is committed to or strategically delegating tasks and roles to be intrinsically aligned to each team member.

One of the strengths of the Team Academy programmes is the numerous opportunities, ad hoc events, and challenges offered for the students to engage in. These business openings are what makes the programmes a diverse and rich environment of entrepreneurship learning. Students can experience working with different teams consisting of a very different constellation of members (different constellations of members lead to different team dynamics impacting and shaping leadership practices and approaches each team uses). The leadership processes in each of these teams is a result of interaction between members exhibiting different leadership styles (as discussed earlier), differences in the focus of leadership action (these are often linked to students' values with some members pushing for leadership to prioritize processes, while others accenting people's wellbeing, development of the team's culture, or the product or service etc.), or frequency in leadership contributions (i.e. some team members will contribute more than others by voicing they ideas and opinions more frequently). The variety of opportunities means students can also engage in projects occurring in very different settings e.g. some projects are limited to 24 hours only and by this externally given conditioning, call for situational leadership and more direct style of leading (these 24-hour events are named in the UWE *Out of the Chrysalis* or *Birth Giving* in other Team Academies). Most importantly, each of the opportunities is *real*, i.e. students work with real clients and on real business challenges. The *realness* of the challenges, as well as the sheer number of the openings, propels learners into *inhabiting* situations that were once uncomfortable. Often learners are asked to *stretch* and demonstrate a willingness to learn and be vulnerable, exposing their imperfectness and *do it anyway* so that they can learn quicker and more effectively.

As shared by one of the students, this richness of opportunities means the programme is a bit like:

> … a Leadership Playground. The playground is there, available to you, but you decide on your own whether you enter it or not. It's up to you to say "yes" and engage with the variety of different opportunities, events, and challenges. The freedom of choice is both empowering and scary as it means it's on you, i.e. it's your responsibility and if things don't work out or you didn't get what you wanted you can't blame anyone but yourself. The advice is clear: engage, decide which project you are going to play with, for how long, with whom, and so on and simply play. The great thing is you are not judged on how you "played" but you get feedback. Feedback is not judgment. Feedback is learning. So over years, if you play a lot and often, you learn to play better and better and better. You become more effective, and gain confidence in how to lead and how to best engage in the leadership process. (Student B, 2017)

Where some students might resist learning and do not actively participate in the leadership processes others thrive on the challenges offered to them. When asked about their desire to learn leadership these learners will share they feel supported and encouraged but also that it's simply *safe* to learn even if you don't have much experience. In some teams the desire to *learn* leadership can be so extensive, there might be more than one member expressing interest in taking a formal leadership role within the team. As observed on the Team Entrepreneurship programme in Bristol, often such teams will form a leadership sub-team consisting of all the students interested in leading. This sub-team will be acting as leadership or *progression* sub-team collectively taking the role of directing team's leadership processes (students often resist the word *leadership* and /or *leader* associating it with power, and control and often look to replace these words with a more *gentle* equivalent, like *progression*). Regardless of the existence of such leadership sub-teams (or formally appointed leader/leaders), the structure of the teams on Team Academy programmes stay flat. Leaders are managed and stay accountable to the team with the majority of decisions made by consensus. In a way, due to programme design such that members cannot hire, fire or give bonuses, members are forced to "make it work" and find a way of motivating and engaging everyone in a team with no one having more authority than others, even if with a formal leadership role. At the same, to stay accurate, it might we worth nothing at the UWE students are equipped to give out some form of bonuses in terms of mark variation for their team assignments. Although not the same as financial bonuses, this is sometimes used by teams to reward extra effort or *punish* lack of engagement.

Team Academy-based programmes recognize an act of leadership can be generated by anyone regardless of formal position and beyond formal titles, roles and responsibilities. Students join Team Academy programmes with different levels of readiness to lead and represent very different levels of competence (ability) and confidence (willingness) to engage in the leadership process. It is the programme's unspoken principle everyone has the same right to experiment with leading. This is regardless of the student's natural abilities, or level of previous experience. One of the challenges of the Team Coach is to support and even *shift* a student's perception from *I am unable to lead* to "*I will give it a go*". It is through active participation that students can increase their ability to lead, which in turns increases their confidence and willingness to contribute to future leadership processes and translates into the level of effectiveness of the projects they are working on.

Next to the Team Coaches and the support their provides, it is the culture and values of Team Academy programmes itself contributing to students' level of willingness to experiment with the leadership processes. The Team Academy programmes are like a cradle offering room and safety for students to *play* with leadership. This very particular culture of Team Academy is a key component of learning and builds on a specific language (e.g. no students but Team Entrepreneurs, no teachers but coaches etc.) and methods. Within the numerous tools used on the programme, two seem of particular importance, i.e. dialogue and the circle processes.

All formal discussions between team members occur using circle processes. This means team members sit in a circle with no tables or any other physical obstruction between them (Baldwin, & Linnea, 2010). Everyone in the room is encouraged to voice their views and opinions and communicate using principles of dialogue (Isaacs, 1999). Both of these processes (i.e. circle and dialogue) encourage team members to reach decisions by consensus and respecting the views of all members participating in the process. More than that, they create an atmosphere where all views are important, and all are valued adding to the creation of culture built on mutual respect, trust, openness, and psychological safety. This points towards another key characteristic of the TE environment: relationships.

Most Team Academy-based programmes last for 3 years. During this time, learners grow, develop, and mature both as people and leaders. At first, in the first year, students hardly know each other. Often, they attempt to impress each other and take a position within their teams. With time, their personal and professional relationships become stronger. The greater understanding of each other's strengths and capabilities allows students to delegate tasks and responsibilities suited to each individual, which in turn maintains high motivation and work ethic. This *closeness* which emerges between the students on the programme resembles a sort of family and ultimately allows students to employ a flexible approach to leading and leadership resting on the mutual quality of relationships within their team.

It's worth noting, all leadership contributions, including those that are *silent* shape the leadership process. Silence, regardless whether a sign of *approval,* an *agreement* or apathy or fear to speak out, is still a contributor to a leadership process. Mistakenly, more silent members of the team often can be labelled and categorized as *followers* where others, more vocal and able to articulate their ideas better are named *leaders.* Such labelling, i.e. leader/follower often leads to confusions and contributes to the distorted understanding of leadership as a static phenomenon. As discussed, leadership is a dynamic, fluid process shaped in micro-interactions between all members of the team. The enactment of leadership occurs *in-between* all participants with the roles of leaders and followers in constant flux and each team member acting as both: leader and follower, taking each of these roles at different times and to different degrees. As described by one of the students:

*the challenge is in transition and moving between leading and following, following and leading and so on. It is almost if I do not need to practice how to lead or how to follow but how to shift, competently, between one to another.* (Student A, 2019)

It would be a misconception to believe all leadership action is a positive one. Literature speaks of both a bright and dark side of leadership (Conger, 1990). At Team Entrepreneurship both types of leading are witnessed, but often the dysfunctional examples of leadership are failed to be recognized as leadership itself. In the context of Team Entrepreneurship, the dark side of leading most often springs from a place of ego, the desire of power, lack of awareness or difficulty in letting go, and clinging to one vision or idea. These acts of dark leadership might be particularly difficult for a team coach to facilitate almost calling for direct intervention. In such instances, it is worth reminding oneself it's not the role of the Coach to project their ideas of *what is right.* The focus of the Team Coach action is to support students in generating as much learning as possible and understanding both the *dark* and *bright* sides of leadership is a rich source of learning. The Team Coach almost continuously stands in front of the choice: intervene or not? Partanen (2012), who established the Team Academy model, advices to do this what contradictory, i.e. if you think you should then most probably you should not and vice versa. Another way of working with the concept of intervention and non-intervention is to *trust the process* and allow it to continue remembering the only objective is to support the team and individuals in harvesting the learning, regardless whether the learning is judged as positive, negative, dark or bright, beneficial or not.

Perhaps another interesting element of leadership as occurring in Team Academy-based programmes is that it happens between leaders who are still going through huge brain changes. It must be remembered the majority of students on the programme in Bristol are between the ages of 18 and 22. Their age might have a direct impact on how they respond to challenges, authorities, what style of interaction they prefer or even how many hours of sleep they need each night (Siegel, 2015). Although all Team Academy programmes are based on the same principles, there are noticeable differences between individual programmes. For example, the age of the students across different countries varies, i.e. students on the UK-based programmes are at least a few years younger than students on the Finish programmes (i.e. in the UK is 18–22; in Finland, nearly one-fifth of students starting to study for a university Bachelor's degree are aged 25 or over). The age of the students might impact the characteristics of the leadership processes with learners across different countries engaging in a leadership process differently.

Next to the specific culture of Team Academy programmes, and the relatively young age of the team members, another characteristic of the programmes is its focus, i.e. entrepreneurship. Entrepreneurship was defined by one of the TEs as "making things happen". It can be said entrepreneurs are a *special breed* usually highly creative, open to risk-taking, results and action-oriented. Their natural orientation is on *doing, moving forward* and *creating* with a clear focus on *action* and *achievement.* Some students speak of an *entrepreneurial approach to leadership* and describe it as the leadership of agility, flexibility, and responsiveness to the ever-changing environment. Further, the act of the leadership, i.e. the focus of the leadership action, is shaped by the entrepreneurial opportunity with both leadership and entrepreneurship being in a constant dance with each other. Both business environments, and thus leadership contexts, are dynamic (Renko, 2013) and in constant interplay. To be successful, entrepreneurial leaders must learn to spot the opportunities and act quickly, constantly adapting and altering their leadership to match the shifting environment (Kelley et al., 2002).

Below I present key observations together with leader related learning outcomes.

Key Observation 1
- Leadership can come from anyone and is not restricted to formal roles, titles and responsibilities. For the Team Coach, one of the priorities is to support the culture of psychological safety and encourage a shift in students' perspectives such that each student feels they are entitled to *play* with learning leadership regardless of differences in their natural abilities or level of previous experience.
    Suggested leadership related learning outcome:

    - Student can provide a variety of examples of leadership emergence and reflect on personal beliefs related to their entitlement to lead.


Key Observation 2
- There are a variety of leadership styles and traits of their leadership behaviour. The Team Coach might consider encouraging students to reflect on themselves as a leader and how their style

and traits impacts on the shape of the leadership processes.
Suggested leadership related learning outcome:

* Student able to self-analyse as a leader and draw conclusions
on their observations.

Key Observation 3

* There are at least two sides to leadership. Leaders action can be
aimed both at contributing to moving the team forward or e.g.
manipulating the team's perception to achieve personal gains. The
literature describes these as *bright* and *dark* sides of leadership.
The role of the Team Coach is to support the Team members with
harvesting learning regardless of the type of leadership present in
their teams.
Suggested leadership related learning outcome:

* Student able to distinguish between dark and bright leadership and how each can generate learning for both the
individual and the team.

Key Observation 4

* The Team Academy programmes are aimed at young people going
through extensive brain developmental changes. The students' age
might shape leadership behaviour displayed in a team. Similarly,
learners' identity of entrepreneur further contributes to and shapes
leadership processes. Both, the age of the students as well as their
entrepreneurial spirit, should be kept at the forefront of the Team
Coach coaching interventions.
Suggested leadership learning:

* Student able to reflect and describe how their entrepreneurial
identity and age might relate to their style of leading.

Key Observation 5

* There are multiple opportunities to experiment with the concept of
leadership on the Team Academy-based programmes. There are
entrepreneurial projects, but also self-generated initiatives and
other events offered by the programme. The variations in learning
opportunities offered to students remain the key advantage of the
Team Academy-based programmes as it enables students not only
*learn* about leadership but also *experiment* with it over and over
again. This leadership richness of opportunities should be

sustained across the Team Academy-based programmes.
Suggested leadership related learning outcome:

- Student able to describe and compare leadership processes used across many different entrepreneurial opportunities.

## Key Observation 6

- The culture of Team Academy-based programmes is a key element of supporting leadership learning. This culture is built on the use of particular tools and methods such as coaching, dialogue and circle processes, and as a result, leading towards increased psychological safety. This is another key area for the Team Coach to support the emergence of a culture where leadership can be safely experimented with, where students allow themselves to be vulnerable and open up to leadership action, regardless of their inexperience or lack of abilities.
  Suggested leadership related learning outcome:

- Student able to reflect on how a culture based on coaching, dialogue, and circle processes impacts the leadership processes.

## Key Observation 7

- Each team member shapes the process of collective leadership. These include members who do not voice or seem to be participating in the leadership process actively.
  Suggested leadership related learning outcome:

- Students reflect on how leadership inaction shapes the leadership processes.

## Key Observation 8

- Any collective process relies on the qualities and strengths of its singular elements. These singular elements are the individual team members. The role of the Team Coach is double-edged: to *strengthen* the collective process of leadership as occurring in the team as well as *strengthen* the team's individual parts through self-discovery, mastery and self-leadership.
  Suggested leadership related learning outcome:

- Student able to reflect on their own leader's development and growth.

## Conclusion

This chapter focused on exploring the concept of a leader in the Team Academy. Numerous theories had been introduced and briefly discussed. These were then applied to the context, in particular, Team Entrepreneurship programme based in Bristol. The key observations had been shared with suggested leader related learning outcomes.

Next to sharing observations related to the concept of a leader as in the entrepreneurial teams, this short introduction was aimed at starting a dialogue on the topic so that further perspectives and observations can be shared, gathered, and discussed.

Future research might in particular focus on exploring the concept of leadership as developing in interaction with progressing team development. Another interesting angle would be to look at how leadership is perceived by young team entrepreneurs.

It is hoped this chapter inspires, challenges, and encourages further discussion on the concept of the leader in the context of the Team Academy programmes.

## Note

1 I noted these reflections in my notebooks – they are not published anywhere. They are written by hand; part of my reflective journals from sessions or 1-2-1.

## References

Avolio, B. J. (1999). *Full leadership development: Building the vital forces in organizations*. London: Sage.

Avolio, B. J., & Gardner, W. L. (2005). Authentic leadership development: Getting to the root of positive forms of leadership. *The Leadership Quarterly, 16*(3), 315–338.

Baldwin, C., & Linnea, A. (2010). *The circle way: A leader in every chair*. Oakland, CA: Berrett-Koehler Publishers.

Bass, B. M., & Avolio, B. J. (Eds). (1994). *Improving organizational effectiveness through transformational leadership*. London: Sage.

Bass, B. M., & Bass Bernard, M. (1985). *Leadership and performance beyond expectations*. New York: The Free Press.

Boyatzis, R. E., Boyatzis, R., & McKee, A. (2005). *Resonant leadership: Renewing yourself and connecting with others through mindfulness, hope, and compassion*. Harvard, MA: Harvard Business Press.

Carsten, M. K., & Uhl-Bien, M. (2013). Ethical followership: An examination of followership beliefs and crimes of obedience. *Journal of Leadership & Organizational Studies, 20*(1), 49–61.

Carsten, M. K., Uhl-Bien, M., West, B. J., Patera, J. L., & McGregor, R. (2010). Exploring social constructions of followership: A qualitative study. *The Leadership Quarterly, 21*(3), 543–562.

Conger, J. A. (1990). The dark side of leadership. *Organizational Dynamics, 19*(2), 44–55.

Cummings, G. G., Tate, K., Lee, S., Wong, C. A., Paananen, T., Micaroni, S. P., & Chatterjee, G. E. (2018). Leadership styles and outcome patterns for the nursing workforce and work environment: A systematic review. *International Journal of Nursing Studies, 85*, 19–60.

De Raad, B. (2000). *The big five personality factors: The psycholexical approach to personality.* Boston, MA: Hogrefe & Huber Publishers.

George, B. (2016). The rise of true north leaders. *Leader to Leader, 2016*(79), 30–35.

Goleman, D., Boyatzis, R. E., & McKee, A. (2002). *The new leaders: Transforming the art of leadership into the science of results.* London: Sphere.

Goleman, D., Welch, S., & Welch, J. (2012). *What makes a leader?* (pp. 93–102). New York: Findaway World, LLC.

Isaacs, W. (1999). *Dialogue and the art of thinking together: A pioneering approach to communicating in business and in life.* NYC: Broadway Business.

Judge, T. A., & Bono, J. E. (2000) Five-factor model of personality and transformational leadership. *Journal of Applied Psychology, 85*(5), 751.

Kelley, W. M., Macrae, C. N., Wyland, C. L., Caglar, S., Inati, S., & Heatherton, T. F. (2002). Finding the self? An event-related fMRI study. *Journal of Cognitive Neuroscience, 14*(5), 785–794.

Kouzes, J. M., & Posner, B. Z. (2008). We lead from the inside out. *The Journal of Values-Based Leadership, 1*(1), 5.

Organ, D. W. (1996). Leadership: The great man theory revisited. www.thefreelibrary.com

Partanen, J. (2012). *The team coach's best tools.* Jyväskylä: Partus.

Pranis, K. (2015). *Little book of circle processes: A new/old approach to peacemaking.* New York: Simon and Schuster.

Renko, M. (2013). Early challenges of nascent social entrepreneurs. *Entrepreneurship Theory and Practice, 37*(5), 1045–1069.

Rus, D., van Knippenberg, D., & Wisse, B. (2010). Leader self-definition and leader self-serving behavior. *The Leadership Quarterly, 21*(3), 509–529.

Siegel, D. J. (2015). *Brainstorm: The power and purpose of the teenage brain.* London: Penguin.

# Concluding Thoughts: Contributors' Conversation

*Elinor Vettraino and Berrbizne Urzelai*

Throughout this book, you will have met a number of researchers, practitioners, and learners all working with the Team Academy model and philosophy of entrepreneurial team learning. What follows is an amalgamation of a number of conversations that have taken place over the development of this book with many of the contributors, along with responses to some core questions about the place and purpose of leadership and teams within the TA model. To help focus the thinking about the model, we invited authors to consider responses to questions around what has surprised them about the way in which learners have engaged with leadership, what makes a TA-based team different from other teams, and what might the challenges of team-based learning post COVID be. The emerging conversations that follow offer an indication of some of the contributors' thoughts about the model and approach.

| | |
|---|---|
| *Elinor Vettraino:* | I wanted to start with thinking about how you have experienced leadership in the TA work that you do? What have been the surprising elements for you working with learners in the model? |
| *Pete Tasi:* | I think one of the main things that surprised me has been the tendency of team entrepreneurs (TEs) to seek leadership from the team coaches and the shyness with which the topic is approached. In the team companies, all TEs are on the same level – there is no hierarchy and I think this causes confusion, especially in the first year of a team. |
| *Hugo Gaggiotti:* | Yes, something we observed was how the TEs might be frustrated by the team coach's refusal |

DOI: 10.4324/9781003163121-102

|                        |                                                                                                                                                                                                                                                                                                                                              |
| ---------------------- | -------------------------------------------------------------------------------------------------------------------------------------------------------------------------------------------------------------------------------------------------------------------------------------------------------------------------------------------- |
|                        | to *lead* their learning from the position of expert.                                                                                                                                                                                                                                                                                         |
| *Elinor:*              | That's an interesting point, Hugo. Pete, you mentioned confusion earlier and I wonder why do you think that confusion occurs?                                                                                                                                                                                                                 |
| *Pete:*                | I think we are used to hierarchical systems in which someone has a formal authority and takes the lead. It was super interesting to see that in 2018, the first year of our [Team Academy Bremerhaven] opening, TEs were all the time asking us, as the team coaches for leadership on many levels.                                             |
| *Ann-Cathrin Scheider:* | Yes, this really made us realize that the process of unlearning is of critical importance when it comes to leadership in team academies. Unlearning can happen in the form of questioning our *taken for granted* assumptions. So, after the teams questioned their beliefs about leadership, we saw that informal leadership consolidated into formal leadership. |
| *Berrbizne Urzelai:*   | That's interesting. So, the need to have some form of formalized leadership did occur but it began through informal means?                                                                                                                                                                                                                    |
| *Ann-Cathrin:*         | Yes, the need for a management team on the team company level opens this process. However, the leadership in teams remains flexible and the programme supports a rotation of the leadership roles every 6 months. In this way, everyone in the team company theoretically has the chance to take on a leadership role.                          |
| *Carol Jarvis:*        | When they first join the Sports Business & Entrepreneurship programme, many TEs imagine leaders and leadership as something performed by heroic individuals and most don't see themselves in this role and nor do they want to appoint as *leader* someone they see as an equal. Leadership is almost a *dirty* word!                           |
| *Berrbizne:*           | It's interesting you mention the need for management, Ann-Cathrin, because I ask the TEs a lot about the difference between                                                                                                                                                                                                                    |

management and leadership, the leadership style they feel comfortable with, etc. so somehow I am encouraging them to explore the concepts and come back to the leadership meetings having read something so that we discuss where they position themselves and how they want to set up goals around their *leadership experience* in the team company.

Pete: I think what you are saying Berrbizne relates to a persistent challenge for TEs which is about *how much leadership can I take? Will the others still like me if I take the lead? How do I lead a team of equals?* All those questions can only be solved by testing different leadership approaches and this process is sometimes very slow, as TEs are shy to take the lead. It seems that many assumptions around leadership have a negative connotation. It is a process to lead and sometimes it is surprising that we talk about leadership like it was a natural capacity. Instead, it is an art that our TEs have the chance to learn during their studies.

Amaia Aranceta: I agree, and our learners don't always understand that leaders are not necessarily authoritarian figures! Transparency in leadership is a quality that our learners develop because we feel that skills that a leader must have are important to understand from a humanistic perspective. As they get experience, they quickly understand a leader's role inside and organization and a team, but the concept requires a longitudinal understanding of how organizations and teams develop.

Selen Kars: We also observed that as the TEs engaged more with the process of leading, an appreciation that leadership can take many different forms and emerge from many different places occurred. As they experience leadership in their teams, they stop seeing leadership as something *done* by one individual to others to trigger task behaviour in others. Instead, they start recognizing leadership as a group activity that works through and within relations.

*Carol:* Yes, the idea that everyone leads together and at the same time.

*Berrbizne:* I also find that when TEs are not encouraged to explore what leadership or management is or is not given relevant or appropriate feedback around that, they end up interpreting *leadership* in their own particular way. For instance, from my perspective, they seem to be quite confused about what shared leadership means, and also what followership is in relation to leadership because not everyone will lead a team. In fact, we have that as one of the elements in our competency framework so that they know we have the expectation that they will consider these concepts, both from learning by doing and learning from others, for example, reading.

*Heikki:* One of the things that has surprised me as a coach is the capability of the TEs to lead themselves, and to create a culture of leadership within a Team Academy.

*Elinor:* That's great to hear, Heikki, because I often think that self-leadership is, I feel, one of the biggest challenges that the TEs face – and the coaches too, I think. I always start with the idea of being able to *fit your own oxygen mask first, before fitting others* as a way of explaining self-leadership to them because that is an angle I think the TEs don't really consider. But I also think the focus on this is what makes TA teams different from other teams. In a TA team, there is a need to understand yourself and your way of being in relation to others, because you are trying to advance your teammates and not just yourself. That's a bit different, I think.

*Heikki:* Yes, Team Academy teams are learning teams with the project teams. The teams become the tools or vehicles for individual learning to take place.

| | |
|---|---|
| *Amaia:* | Yes, so a TA team differs from other teams because of the way that their everyday work and learning processes are done. Teams are based on collaborative work and the TEs learn by experimentation. In Mondragon Team Academy (MTA) it is important for us that our teams engage in cooperation, interaction, and experimentation from day 1 to enable them to complete their academic projects. |
| *Carol:* | You mention collaboration Amaia, and I would say that one thing that would benefit further exploration is the nuanced engagement that we have observed with the notions of *collaboration* and *competition*. We found that in different situations, teams might find themselves collaborating and competing with each other and sometimes simultaneously which is interesting. In TA teams, collaboration encourages the team to put everyone's talent to the best use, and competition encourages them to give their best. |
| *Berrbizne:* | Yes, the two can go hand-in-hand. On a different note, but something I think it is important that we acknowledge because it impacts on how the teams function; in many Team Academies, the teams are formed by the programme staff or coaching teams. |
| *Ann-Cathrin:* | Yes, we are the same. The process of team formation is just the reverse of what usually happens in real life. Entrepreneurial teams are created when a common goal already exists in the background, which is why the business itself is created, and this also presupposes that the team members already know each other. On the other hand, in a TA, we form teams from people who were previously unfamiliar to each other and then engage in newly created, artificial teams to start a business together. This is suggested also from our website in Bremerhaven: http://unternimm-doch-was.de/, *do something entrepreneurial.* |

| | |
|---|---|
| *Berrbizne:* | We also do personality tests, motivation-related tests, and collect information about the TEs' hobbies, skills, background, etc. in their motivation letters. And we also observe them during induction and take notes about their engagement, interaction with others, and so on so that we can create teams which are as *diverse* as possible. |
| *Elinor:* | I agree, Ann-Cathrin, that the process is backwards! Setting up a team without a central theme or passion is definitely a challenge, but that is where some of the best learning occurs. I think we also operate a similar process Bremerhaven and UWE, although we don't have a requirement that TEs *have* to create businesses. Instead, we focus on the generation of value creation through a range of possible activities, including business formation if allowed,[1] and the concept of the broader team being a *learning organization* in which the smaller project teams and businesses can develop. |
| *Berrbizne:* | Yes, I have seen that in some TAs where the focus is more on the *learning organization* side of things: sharing knowledge and experiences and providing support, whereas others are solely focused on the *business/company set up* side. I think we should do both because one complements the other. |
| *Elinor:* | Both require a shared team vision or strategy though. |
| *Berrbizne:* | Yes, all teams have a *team strategy* behind what they do: goals, mission, vision, values. I think this is not only in TA teams, though, it is in any team. Also, we haven't mentioned team size yet, and I think that is a difference. |
| *Pete:* | That is true. In Bremerhaven, the team companies have about 15 people in them. |
| *Berrbizne:* | That is a bit different from UWE. We can have up to 20 members in a team, but I think in other TAs they can have very few? |

Elinor:

Yes, that's true! In TA Aston, as we are a very new TA, we have a third-year team comprising three TEs! Very small indeed. With both challenges and benefits. In TA Lincoln, our first team entered the third year as a trio and worked extremely effectively together because there was less difference. However, the challenge with such small teams is that there is little opportunity for a breadth of experience and shared learning.

Pete:

Yes, but in a team of 15, problems and tensions naturally appear … .

Berrbizne:

… and a complaint we often hear is that teams can't *hire* or *fire* members!

Elinor:

Very true! Although that does happen in some of the Finnish TAs. One of many *joyful challenges* that exist for both TEs and team coaches alike! And talking of challenges, the world post COVID will see considerable change for all. What do you foresee as being the toughest challenges for team-based learning approaches to come, and how might we overcome these?

Hugo:

I think this is a tricky question because participating in a coaching session is an embodied experience that can't be entirely replicated in a hybrid virtual face-to-face environment, which seems to be a taken-for-granted practice in post COVID learning environments. There isn't a simple answer to this question because the experience will be different for everyone.

Amaia:

This is true, and obviously COVID has created limitations that MTA have not faced before but we have adapted our learning methodology to the situation, and I think we will continue to enable the progress of our students by taking necessary measures moving forward. However, I think that one of the main challenges for the future will be overcoming social distancing to ensure we can re-create the pre-COVID standards of team working.

*Berrbizne:* Yes, obviously the remote and online working experience we have had this past year has influenced the formation stage, particularly of our year 1 teams. And they might have suffered a bit more in terms of creating a bond and getting to know the wider TE community. But they have also learned to be more flexible and adaptable, and resilient, and I think that they will overcome the challenges they face with their experience, way of organizing themselves, and how they share capacity to learn and work together.

*Selen:* Certainly, more established teams have typically found it less difficult to keep up momentum than new starts have found to generate it, and that really highlights the importance of relationships and activities outside of training sessions and organized activities. This could be the case in the future.

*Ann-Cathrin:* I agree. Creating a new *new-normal* will be the biggest challenge. If you had told me that we could shift a TA process fully online, I would have laughed out loud! But it works, and it works well. In our team coaching team, we are already talking about which elements can remain in online formats and which we want to do offline. And by assessing as much as possible in advance, we hope we can make the transition faster and enable creative thinking to occur.

*Elinor:* I completely agree, Ann-Cathrin! We are doing the same. The fully virtual Global Business Challenge (GBC$^2$) which was set up by a group of us in the summer of 2020 has added tremendous value to the participants' learning, and it is not only here to stay as a core part of many of the participating institutions' programmes of study, it is growing.

| | |
|---|---|
| *Pete:* | It's a great initiative, the GBC! I think that another challenge post COVID will also potentially be that some TEs won't be living in the cities that their universities are based in anymore, and in these cases, we may have to consider that individual teams need individual solutions. We will definitely need to build resilience! For the TES, the teams, and the team coaches. |
| *Elinor:* | Resilience! Definitely needed for all. Heikki, any closing thoughts? |
| *Heikki:* | Yes, it is difficult, but the strong community will carry on even in remote circumstances. I have no doubts about that! |

As is quite often the case, at the end of our discussions in this book, which is the third in the series, we were left with more questions to consider about how leadership and teams are evolving as concepts within the context of TA. Rather than being the end of the story, this is very much part of the journey. Book 1: *Team Academy in Entrepreneurship Education* in this series explores the underpinning philosophy of TA, where it began and how it relates to the broader team coaching and entrepreneurial learning work taking place. Book 2: *Team Academy in Practice* focuses on how TA appears in practice, exploring research and narratives from those in the field who are working with and developing academic TA-based programmes of study. The final book, Book 4: *Team Academy in Diverse Settings*, completes this series' journey considering how TA appears outside of traditional TA-based settings, considering how TA might work in industry, schools, communities of practice and beyond, and the legacy that it has left in learners and practitioners. There are many more stories to be told, and certainly more research to be done into this emergent model. Join us to further the conversation!

## Notes

1 International students studying in the UK have restrictions imposed on them by the UK Government relating to what business activity they can and cannot do. One of the restrictions is that they are not allowed to set up and run companies, to be directors or shareholders of companies, or to profit from them. In order to support international students to engage in our programmes at Aston University, we don't stipulate that all students must set up and run companies and, in fact, they can engage in relevant and

developmental entrepreneurial activities through placement activity and project work that we encourage.

2 The Global Business Challenge is an international team learning-based programme that enables teams of mixed nationality participants to engage in an 8-week-long real-world client challenge as a learning experience. The first GBC occurred between October and December 2020 and involved over 110 learners from six universities, in four countries. The third round will involve 200 learners from eight universities, in six countries. For more information on how to be involved, contact Dr Elinor Vettraino (e.vettraino@ aston.ac.uk).

# Index

Note: Page numbers followed by "n" refer to notes; and page numbers in *Italic* refer to figures and page numbers in **bold** refer to tables.